W9-AND-555

SIMPLY THE BEST
GARNISHING SET RECIPES

MARIAN GETZ

INTRODUCTION BY WOLFGANG PUCK

ACKNOWLEDGMENTS

A most sincere thank you to our wonderful viewers and customers for without you there would be no need for a cookbook. I try very hard to give you an array of recipes suited for the particular kitchen tool the cookbook is written for. Wolfgang and I create recipes faster than we can write them down. That is what chefs do and is also the reason to tune in to the live shows and even record them so you can learn new dishes that may not be in our cookbooks yet.

Thank you most of all to Wolfgang. You are the most passionate chef I know and it has been a privilege to work for you since 1998. You are a great leader and friend. Your restaurants are full of cooks and staff that have been with you for 20 or more years which is a true testament to how you lead us. Thanks for allowing me to write these cookbooks and for letting me share the stage at HSN with you.

To Greg, my sweet husband since 1983. Working together is a dream and I love you. You have taught me what a treasure it is to have a home filled with people to laugh with.

To my sons, Jordan and Ben, we have a beautiful life, don't we? It just keeps on getting better since we added Lindsay, J. J. and now precious Easton, our first grandbaby.

To all the great people at WP Productions, Syd, Arnie, Mike, Phoebe, Michael, Nicolle, Tracy, Genevieve, Gina, Nancy, Sylvain, Rodney and the rest of the team, you are all amazing to work with. Watching all the wonderful items we sell develop from idea to final product on live television is an awe-inspiring process to see and I love that I get to be a part of it.

To Daniel Koren, our patient editor and photographer, thank you for your dedication. You make the photo shoot days fun and you are such an easygoing person to work with in the cramped, hot studio we have to share. We have learned so much together and have far more to learn.

To Greg, Cat, Estela, Angi, J.J., Laurie and Tomasa who are the most dedicated, loving staff anyone could wish for. You are the true heroes behind the scenes. You are a well-oiled machine of very hard working people who pull off the live shows at HSN. It is a magical production to watch, from the first box unpacked, to the thousands of eggs cracked and beaten to running to get that "thing" Wolf asks for at the last minute, to the very last dish washed and put away it is quite a sight to behold. I love you all and I deeply love what we do.

It is often said that you eat with your eyes first. Whether in my restaurants or at home, I believe that food presentation is a big part of how we experience our meals. The garnishing set will empower you to be more adventurous in the kitchen. Not only will you be able to prepare your food quicker, but also give it a decorative touch that will turn a great dish into an extraordinary experience.

When I asked Marian to write the cookbook for the garnishing set, I knew she would rise to the occasion. Her experience as a pastry chef, wife, mother, and now a grandmother allowed Marian to put together a garnishing cookbook with a wide variety of recipes that I'm sure you will use for years to come.

A student of cooking is probably one of the best ways to describe Marian. She is always looking for something new, something fresh, something local, something seasonal. Her culinary knowledge combined with her passion for cooking is second to none. The recipes that Marian has written for this cookbook will motivate you to be more creative in the kitchen.

As I learned long ago, alongside my mother and grandmother, you should always put lots of love into everything you cook. This is certainly evident in this cookbook.

Wolfgang Puck

TABLE OF CONTENTS

RECIPES

GARNISHING TIPS

Here is a list of my favorite garnishing tools and how I use them everyday for food prep as well as to create memorable fruit displays.

DUAL FLUTED AND ROUND MELON BALLER

Use to hollow out apples and fill with melon balls for an attractive place card holder. Make beautiful fruit salads with an extra special touch. Portion cookie dough and ice cream mini balls with ease. Remove seeds from a long cucumber half in one quick pass. Use fluted side to make fruit baskets that will have everyone talking. Scoop balls from soft cheese for a beautiful relish tray.

SPIRAL SLICER

Use to create effortless spirals from any firm root vegetables such as carrots or radishes to garnish a salad or vegetable tray. Impress your friends and family by serving Tornado Potato chips (see page 54).

DUAL FLUTED SCOOP

Use to create a more delicate scalloped pattern on all melons. Create beautiful ruffled flowers out of radishes and turnips for a truly special garnish that will have everyone taking out their cell phone cameras and asking "How did you do that?"

DUAL CITRUS ZESTER/CHANNEL KNIFE

Use to make beautiful decorative cucumber cups. Make citrus curls for truly memorable cocktails. Use to draw on carved pumpkins and all melons for an easy and quick design. Also great for decorating lemon cupcakes or pies.

CRINKLE CUTTER

Use to turn store-bought pound cake into elegant finger sandwiches. Crinkle cut white and sweet potatoes for the kids. Since it is nice and sharp, use it just like a santoku knife and watch it glide through food effortlessly because of the ripples. Also great to cut carrots, zucchini and even mozzarella cheese into decorative pieces for a special relish platter.

WIRE SLICER

Use to slice tomatoes, hard boiled eggs and fresh mozzarella cheese to make uniform slices all the way through.

SERRATED V-SLICER

Use to carve an attractive edge into watermelon, cantaloupe, honeydew, papaya, kiwi and many other fruits and vegetables. Make stuffed tomatoes that have a special look. Carve pumpkins for Halloween with ease. Create a decorative border in a round loaf of bread then fill with spinach dip.

CERAMIC Y-PEELER

Use this ultra sharp, ceramic blade to effortlessly peel potatoes, carrots, cucumbers and even tomatoes. Peel carrots and tomatoes in a spiral fashion to make roses for a beautiful presentation. Use to make elegant scrolls of chocolate over store-bought chocolate pudding. Great for making restaurant style curls of Parmesan cheese over spaghetti.

APPLE CORER

Use to core apples, pineapple, tomatoes and so much more. Core out cupcakes then fill with a surprise before frosting the tops. Use to make eyes and other decorations on carved melons. Core pineapple slices for a holiday ham or carve a pretty hole pattern into a Jack-O-Lantern for a pretty yet simple presentation (see page 62).

MEDIUM GRATER

Use to grate fresh coconut over curry, Parmesan over lasagna, cheese over tacos or even chocolate over a cream pie. Use on potatoes for latkes or grate vegetables to sneak them into your meatloaf for an extra serving of veggies for picky kids. Grate onions for a milder taste or grate tomato halves all the way down to the skin for a beautiful sauce or salsa.

HERB SHEARS

Triple-quick snip through herbs to garnish foods. Wow your guests during holidays by finishing the turkey presentation with paper frill booties like you see in fancy magazines (see page 76). Use to shred sensitive correspondence that would otherwise require an electric shredder. Make beautiful flowers from leeks that look just like chrysanthemum.

PANTRY TIPS

Being prepared to cook the recipes in this book, or any recipe for that matter, is one of the keys to success in the kitchen. Your pantry must be stocked with the basics. We all know how frustrating it can be when you go to the cupboard and what you need is not there. This list includes some of the ingredients you will find in this book and some that we feel are important to always have on hand.

PERISHABLES:

Onions
Garlic
Tomatoes
Carrots
Celery
Ginger
Bell Peppers
White Potatoes
Sweet Potatoes
Squashes
Citrus
Apples
Bananas
Lettuce
Spinach
Fresh Herbs
Green Onions
Milk
Cream Cheese
Parmesan Cheese
Yogurt
Other Cheeses You Like

SPICES:

Kosher Salt
Pepper
Bay Leaves
Sage
Oregano
Thyme
Chili Flakes
Cumin Seeds
Curry Powder
Onion Powder
Garlic Powder
Dry Mustard
Ground Cinnamon
Nutmeg
Cloves
Chili Powder

DRY GOODS:

Sugars
Sugar Substitute
Vanilla
Extracts/Flavorings
Agave Syrup
Canned Tomatoes
Canned Beans
Canned Vegetables
Dried Chilies
Pasta
Lentils
Stocks
Powdered Bouillon
Olives
Ketchup
Mustard
Pickles
Oils
Vinegar
Honey

It is not necessary to have all the items listed at all times. However, if you are feeling creative, adventurous or just following a recipe, it's great to have a good selection in the kitchen.

EASTER BUNNY BASKET

Makes 4-6 servings

Ingredients:

1 large honeydew melon
1 wedge seedless watermelon
1/2 cantaloupe
1 pint blueberries
1 carrot
1/2 cup red grapes
2 limes

Method:

1. *Trim a small slice off the honeydew melon bottom so it sits flat.*
2. *Use a bamboo skewer to outline the bunny pattern (A).*
3. *Use a knife to cut out the bunny pattern (B).*
4. *Use the **DUAL MELON BALLER** to scoop balls from the honeydew melon, watermelon and cantaloupe.*
5. *For the bunny's eyes, use small pieces of bamboo skewer to attach 2 blueberries to the front of the bunny's face.*
6. *Use the **Y-PEELER** to peel the carrot then use a knife to cut the carrot into long whiskers.*
7. *Secure the whiskers to the bunny's face using additional bamboo skewer pieces (C).*
8. *Fill the bunny's body with fruit.*
9. *Use a knife to slice the limes into thin wheels and arrange around the bunny before serving.*

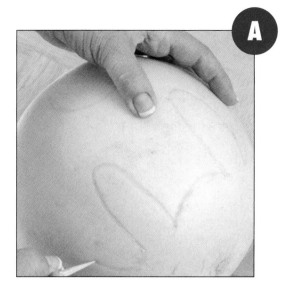

A

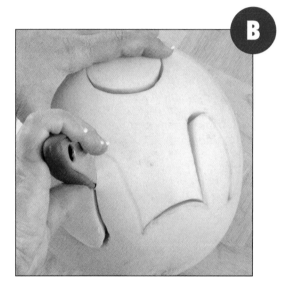

B

C

APPLE FLOWER
PLACE CARD HOLDER

Makes 3 holders

Ingredients:

3 apples
1 wedge cantaloupe
1 wedge honeydew melon
1 wedge watermelon
1 small bunch red grapes
1 small bunch green grapes
1/2 cup blueberries

Method:

1. *Use a knife to cut the bottom off each apple so they sit flat.*
2. *Use the **CHANNEL KNIFE** to pull a double row around each apple (A).*
3. *Cut each apple in half by using a knife between the pulled double rows (B).*
4. *Use the **DUAL MELON BALLER** to scoop out the bottom half of each apple (C).*
5. *Use the **DUAL MELON BALLER** to scoop balls from the cantaloupe, honeydew and watermelon then fill the bottom apple halves with the scooped balls and remaining ingredients (D).*
6. *Use the **DUAL FLUTED SCOOP** to add a decorative border to the top half of each apple (E).*
7. *Place the apple tops over the fruit then secure in place using a wooden toothpick.*
8. *Using a knife, cut a slit into the top of each apple then insert the name cards before serving (F).*

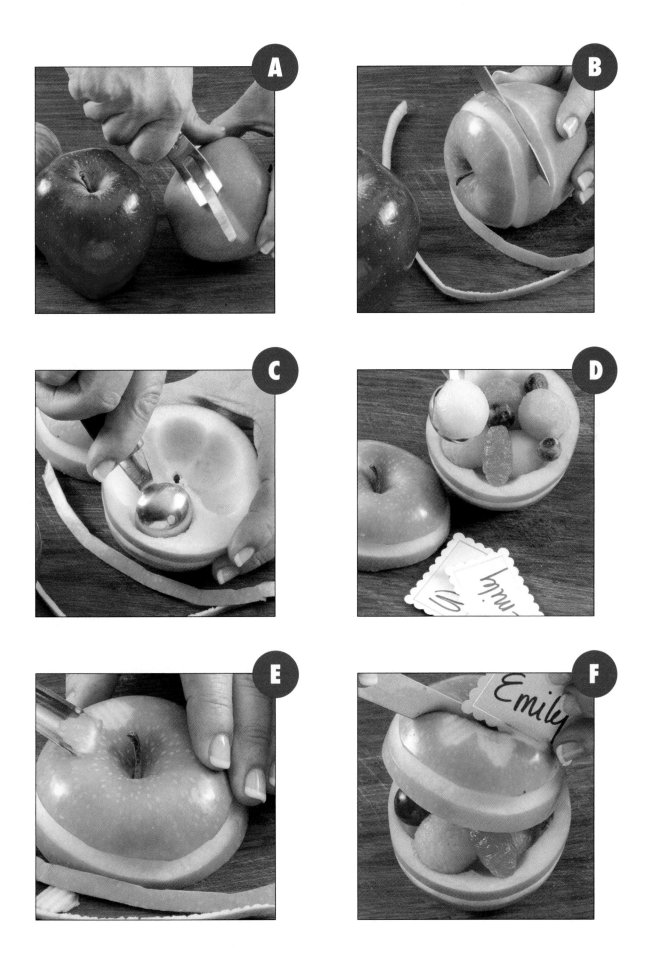

11

PENGUIN ICE TRAY

Makes 8-10 servings

Ingredients:

1 eggplant
1 carrot
1 hard boiled egg
1 head romaine lettuce
2 pounds shrimp, cooked
A few parsley sprigs
1 cup bottled cocktail sauce

Method:

1. *Fill a small and large cookware pot or cake pan with 2-inches of water then freeze the day before serving this ice tray.*
2. *Use a knife to cut the bottom off the eggplant so it sits flat (A).*
3. *Use a knife to cut a slice off the front length to create the penguin's "tummy" (B).*
4. *Use a knife to cut an upward slice on each side of the tummy to create the "wings", leaving them attached at the top (C).*
5. *Use the **Y-PEELER** to peel the carrot by going around the circumference; reserve the peel and large stem of the carrot (D).*
6. *Use a knife to carve the feet and bow tie from the carrot peel then cut out a beak from the carrot stem.*
7. *Use the **WIRE SLICER** to slice the egg using the non-serrated side of the slicer then cut holes into the center of two egg slices using the **APPLE CORER** (E).*
8. *Use a knife to cut two carrot slices from remaining carrot stem then use the **APPLE CORER** to cut eyeballs from carrot slices; secure the eyeballs and beak to the penguin using wooden toothpicks (F).*
9. *Line a platter with the lettuce then top with the ice you made in the pots.*
10. *Stand penguin on top then arrange the shrimp, parsley and cocktail sauce around the penguin before serving.*

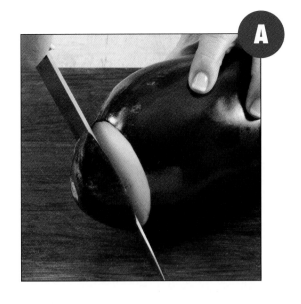

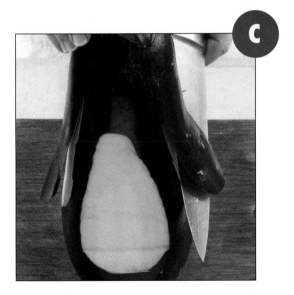

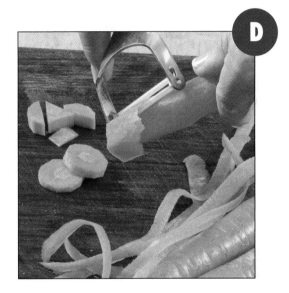

13

HAPPY WHALE

Makes 8-10 servings

Ingredients:

1 large watermelon
1 wedge honeydew melon
1 wedge cantaloupe
3 kiwi
1 wedge pineapple

Method:

1. *Use a large knife to cut the bottom off the watermelon so it sits flat.*
2. *Use a wooden toothpick to trace the eyes and mouth onto one side of the watermelon.*
3. *Use the **APPLE CORER** to create the pupils (A) then use a knife to remove the rind for the eyes around the pupils.*
4. *Use a knife to cut out the mouth, cutting deeper towards the mouth's center to reveal red flesh (B).*
5. *Use a knife to carve a piece of the removed watermelon bottom into the shape of a water spout then use the **Y-PEELER** to remove the rind (C).*
6. *Use a wooden toothpick to trace a tail onto the watermelon on the opposite side of the face (D) then trace around the sides and face; follow the trace with a knife then remove the top by cutting the top into 2 or more pieces to make it easier to remove (E).*
7. *Use the **DUAL MELON BALLER** to scoop melon balls from the melons and cantaloupe.*
8. *Use the **APPLE CORER** to make a blowhole (F) then stick the water spout into the hole.*
9. *Use the **Y-PEELER** to peel the kiwi then use a knife to slice the kiwi and cut pineapple into chunks.*
10. *Add melon balls, kiwi and pineapple to the basket before serving.*

14

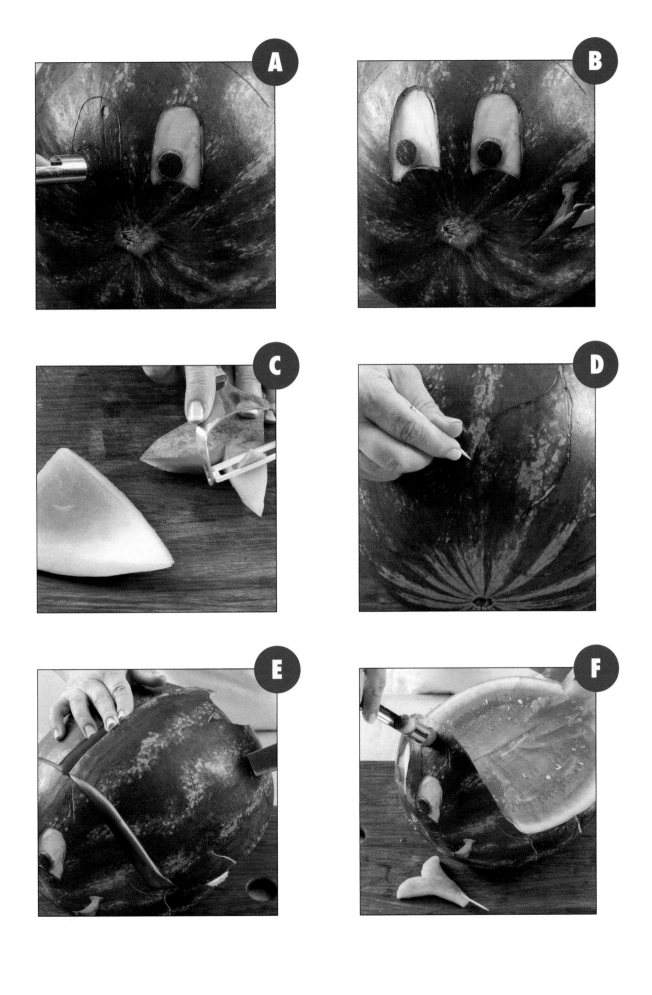

BABY SHOWER
BABY CARRIAGE

Makes 10-15 servings

Ingredients:

1 large watermelon, seedless
1 honeydew melon
1 cantaloupe
1 bunch red grapes
1 bunch green grapes
1 ruby red grapefruit
1 orange

Method:

1. *Use a large knife to cut the bottom off of the watermelon so it sits flat.*
2. *To remove the carriage top, use the **V-SLICER** to cut out the top portion then use a knife to cut around the sides (A).*
3. *Use the **DUAL MELON BALLER** to scoop melon balls from the melons and cantaloupe; set aside.*
4. *Use a knife to cut small slices from the grapes to create the eyes (B).*
5. *Use 3 cantaloupe balls to create the ears and nose (B).*
6. *Use a knife to cut a hole into the grapefruit big enough to hold the pacifier.*
7. *Attach the face components to the grapefruit using small pieces of bamboo skewer.*
8. *Use a knife to cut 4 wheels from the orange.*
9. *Attach orange wheels to the watermelon using pieces of bamboo skewer; add honeydew balls as hubcaps (C).*
10. *Place the grapefruit baby into the carriage then add the melon balls and grapes (D).*
11. *Arrange any extra melon balls or grapes around the carriage before serving.*

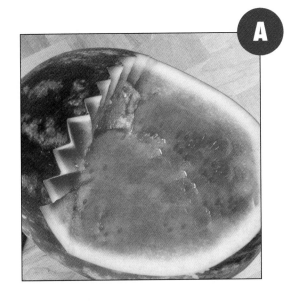

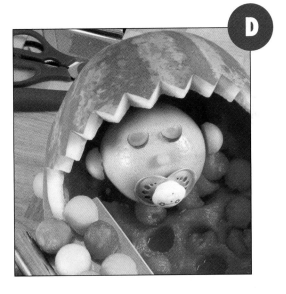

FLOWER VASE

Makes 1 vase

Ingredients:

1 leek
2 turnips
2 radishes
1 carrot
6 green onions
1 butternut squash, hollowed out, flesh reserved
Food coloring

Method:

1. Cut the leek into 2-inch sections; reserve green leaves.
2. Use the **HERB SHEARS** to make cuts on both flat sides of the leeks (A).
3. Place the leeks in water to let the "petals" open (B).
4. Peel the tops off the turnips and radishes then use the **DUAL FLUTED SCOOP** to create petals (C).
5. Place the turnips into water mixed with a few drops of food coloring.
6. Use the **Y-PEELER** to peel the carrot by going around the circumference of the carrot to create petals (D).
7. Secure the leek flowers using wooden skewers inside of the green onions (E); add the reserved leek leaves.
8. Use the **DUAL MELON BALLER** in a circular pattern on a butternut squash creating petals.
9. Create the petal center using the **APPLE CORER** in a colored turnip.
10. Secure the turnip center to the butternut flower using a small wooden toothpick (F).
11. Use a knife to cut the bottom off the butternut squash so it sits flat then use the **DUAL FLUTED SCOOP** to flute the top of the "vase".
12. Use the **CHANNEL KNIFE** to pull decorative patterns around the butternut "vase".
13. Use wooden skewers to arrange the flowers and leek leaves inside the "vase".

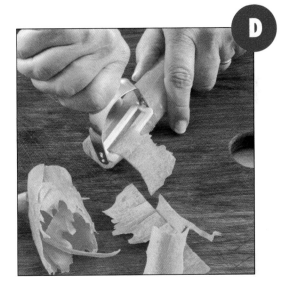

FUN FROGGY

Makes 1 fruit bowl

Ingredients:

1 watermelon
1 wedge cantaloupe
1 wedge honeydew melon
2 black olives

Method:

1. *Use a large knife to cut the bottom off the watermelon so it sits flat.*
2. *Use a large knife to cut out a large V-shaped wedge from the side of the watermelon for the mouth (A).*
3. *Trim the rind off the watermelon wedge.*
4. *Use the **DUAL MELON BALLER** to scoop balls from the watermelon wedge, cantaloupe and honeydew melon.*
5. *Use a knife to cut front and back feet from the rind (B).*
6. *Use a knife to trim eye supports and white of eyes from the rind (C).*
7. *Attach a black olive for the pupil to the white of eye and eye support using a wooden skewer (D); repeat to make a second eye.*
8. *Skewer the eyes into the top of the watermelon (E).*
9. *Fill mouth with melon balls before serving (F).*

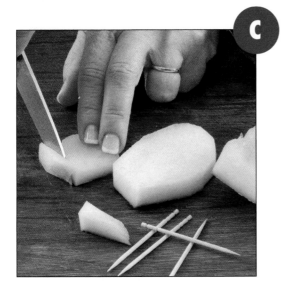

SCHOOL BUS

Makes 6-8 servings

Ingredients:

1 honeydew melon
1 bunch radishes
12 whole cloves
1 small lime
1 pint blueberries
1 pint strawberries
1 pint raspberries
1/4 cup granulated sugar
1/4 cup water
1 teaspoon lemon juice
1/4 teaspoon vanilla extract

FRUIT DISPLAYS

Method:

1. *Use a large knife to cut the bottom off the honeydew melon so it sits flat.*
2. *Use a knife to create windows by carving out four 1/2-inch deep squares on the side of the melon (A).*
3. *Use the **DUAL MELON BALLER** to scoop out the flesh in each window to hold the radishes (B).*
4. *Use the **V-SLICER** to cut an opening on the other side of the honeydew melon (C).*
5. *Reserve all the flesh then use the **DUAL MELON BALLER** to scoop balls from flesh; set aside.*
6. *Select radishes then cut out the mouths using a knife (D).*
7. *Stick two cloves into each of the radishes to make the eyes (E).*
8. *Attach radish heads to the windows of the school bus using pieces of bamboo skewer (F).*
9. *Use a knife to slice 4 wheels from the lime.*
10. *Attach wheels to the sides of the bus using pieces of bamboo skewer; use blueberries for the hubcaps.*
11. *Fill the back of the school bus with the melon balls and remaining fruit.*
12. *Combine the sugar, water, lemon juice and vanilla in a spray bottle.*
13. *Spray the fruit with sugar mixture before serving.*

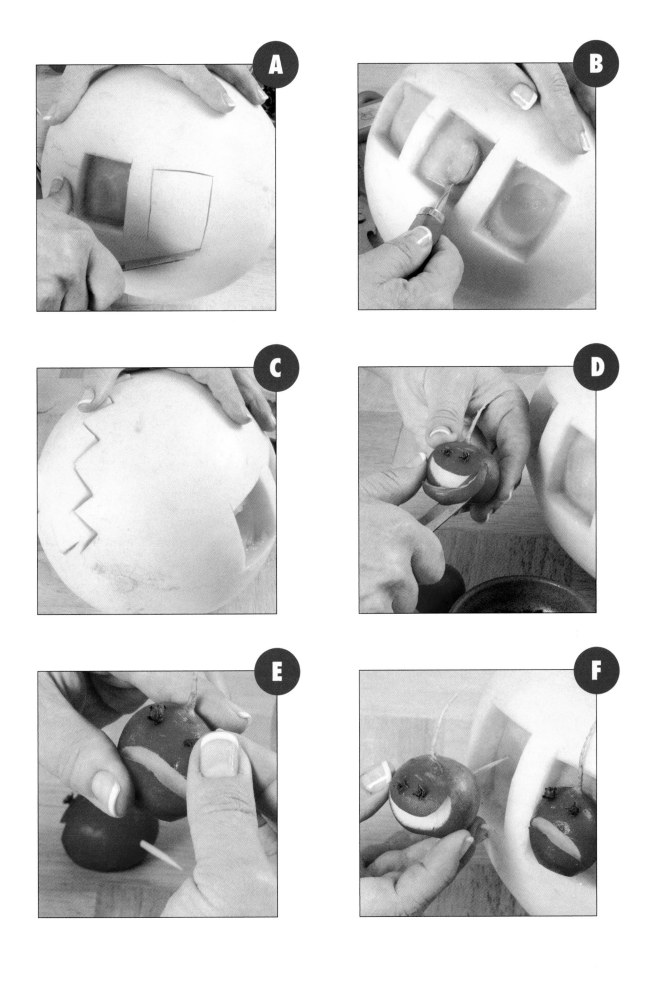

WEDDING SHOWER FRUIT BOWL

Makes 6-8 servings

Ingredients:
1 watermelon, seedless
1 honeydew melon
1 cantaloupe
3 oranges
4 whole cloves
Piece of cheesecloth
Black construction paper and glue
1 pint blueberries
1 bunch red grapes

Method:
1. *Use a large knife to cut the bottom off the watermelon so it sits flat.*
2. *Use a bamboo skewer to trace the car opening into the top of the watermelon.*
3. *Use a knife to cut out the car opening (A); reserve the rind and usable flesh.*
4. *Use a knife to cut a rectangular windshield from the reserved rind (B) then add decorative edges using the* **CHANNEL KNIFE** *(C).*
5. *Use the* **DUAL MELON BALLER** *to scoop balls from the melons and cantaloupe; set aside.*
6. *Use a knife to slice 4 wheels from an orange.*
7. *Attach the wheels to the sides of the watermelon using pieces of bamboo skewer then use melon balls for hubcaps (D).*
8. *Attach "headlights" to the front of the melon using melon balls and pieces of bamboo skewer.*
9. *Use the stem end of each of the remaining oranges as the mouths then attached two cloves to each orange to make the eyes (E).*
10. *Use scissors to cut out a piece of cheesecloth for a veil then use it to cut a hat from the construction paper; glue the hat together.*
11. *Attach the veil and hat to the oranges using pieces of bamboo skewers; use blueberries to create a tiara by attaching to the bamboo skewers holding the veil.*
12. *Attach the windshield to the melon using pieces of bamboo skewer then position the bride and groom behind the windshield (F).*
13. *Fill the car with melon balls, grapes and blueberries before serving.*

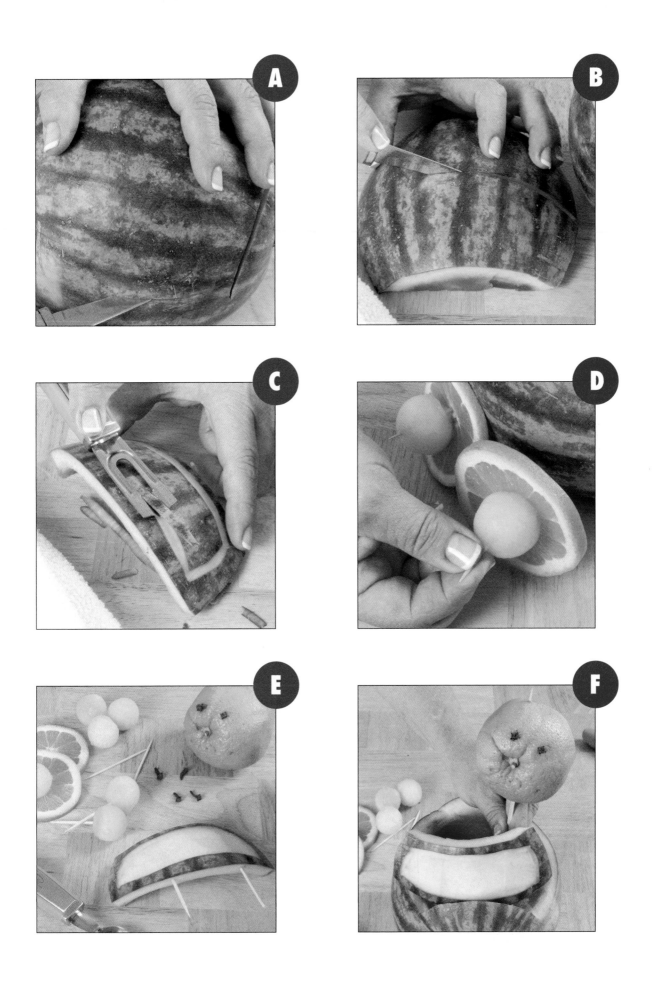

HALLOWEEN
JACK-O-LANTERN

Makes 1 Jack-O-Lantern

Ingredients:
1 small pumpkin
1 glow stick

Method:
1. *Use a knife to cut the bottom off the pumpkin so it sits flat (A).*
2. *Use the **DUAL MELON BALLER** to carve a hole into the pumpkin bottom (B).*
3. *Use a spoon to scoop out the flesh and seeds (C) then scrape the inside walls of the pumpkin until 1/2-inch thick.*
4. *Use the **CHANNEL KNIFE** to pull decorative wavy stripes around the outside of the pumpkin (D & E).*
5. *Use a knife to cut off the pumpkin's top then drop in an activated glow stick (F).*

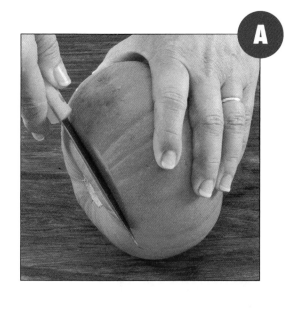

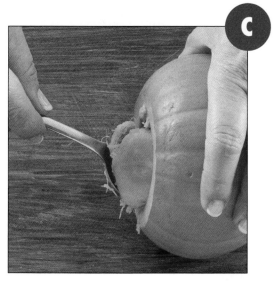

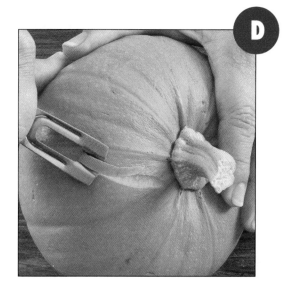

FOURTH OF JULY FRUIT BOWL

Makes 12-15 servings

Ingredients:

1 large watermelon, seedless
1 honeydew melon
1 cantaloupe
3 kiwi
1 package fresh blueberries

Method:

1. Use a large knife to cut the bottom off the watermelon so it sits flat.
2. Use the **CHANNEL KNIFE** to cut the flag's outline and stripes into the side of the watermelon (A & B).
3. Use the **CITRUS ZESTER** to create the stars (B & C).
4. Use a star-shaped cookie cutter and a meat mallet to tap a star on each side of the flag.
5. Use a knife to remove the flesh around the stars.
6. Use a bamboo skewer to outline the basket handle on top of the watermelon (D).
7. Use the **V-SLICER** to cut out the basket area, reserving usable flesh (E).
8. Use the **DUAL MELON BALLER** to scoop balls from the melons and cantaloupe.
9. Use a star-shaped cookie cutter to cut out stars from the melons and cantaloupe (F).
10. Place the stars on long bamboo skewers.
11. Use the **Y-PEELER** to peel the kiwi then slice them using the **CRINKLE CUTTER**.
12. Fill the basket with melon balls, kiwi and blueberries then add the skewered stars.
13. Arrange some additional melon balls around the watermelon to make a decorative border before serving.

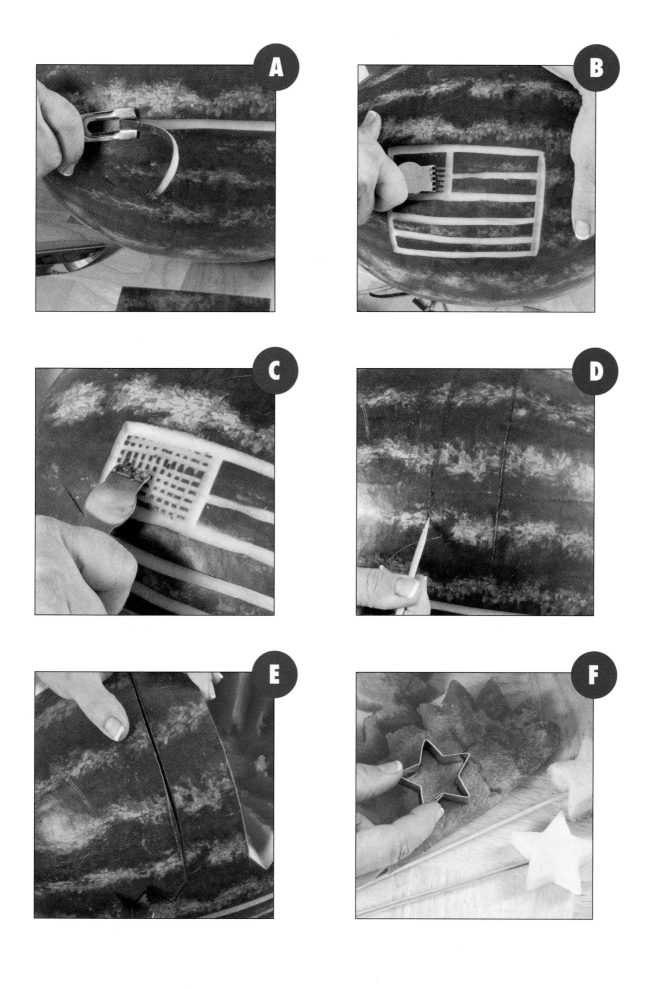

SWEET TEAPOT

Makes 4-5 servings

Ingredients:

1 cantaloupe
1 wedge honeydew melon
1 cup blueberries
The flowers from page 18 (optional)

Method:

1. *Use a knife to cut the bottom off the cantaloupe so it sits flat (A); reserve bottom piece.*
2. *Use the **DUAL FLUTED SCOOP** to make a fluted opening into the top of the cantaloupe (B); reserve the top.*
3. *Use half of the reserved cantaloupe bottom piece to carve out a teapot handle.*
4. *Use the **APPLE CORER** to make a handle opening (C).*
5. *Use the other half of the reserved cantaloupe bottom piece to carve out a spout (D).*
6. *Attach spout and handle to the cantaloupe using wooden toothpicks (E).*
7. *Use both sides of the **DUAL MELON BALLER** to scoop different size melon balls from the cantaloupe and honeydew melon (F).*
8. *Fill the teapot with melon balls and blueberries; place reserved top on the teapot.*
9. *Use a knife to cut a small heart from cantaloupe flesh then attach to the top using a toothpick.*
10. *Arrange additional fruit and the flowers from page 18 around the teapot if desired.*

SPIKY HEDGEHOG

Makes 8-10 servings

Ingredients:
1 large watermelon
3 blueberries

Method:
1. *Use a large knife to cut the bottom off the watermelon so it sits flat (A).*
2. *Use the **V-SLICER** to create the spiky head and opening (B).*
3. *Remove the top portion (C) then use the **CRINKLE CUTTER** to cut all the watermelon flesh into chunks.*
4. *Use the **V-SLICER** to create 4 paws from the removed top portion rind (D).*
5. *Trim a small rind into the shape of a nose then attach a blueberry to the end using a wooden toothpick (E).*
6. *Secure the nose and two blueberries for the eyes to the watermelon using small wooden toothpicks.*
7. *Fill the body with watermelon chunks then add a wooden toothpick to each piece (F).*

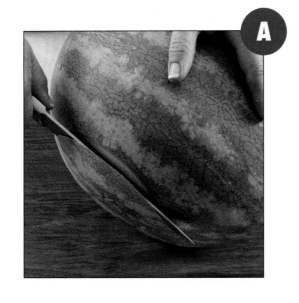

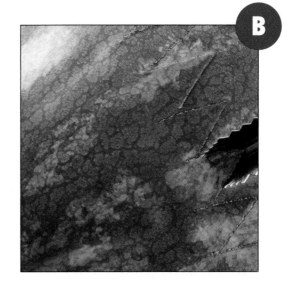

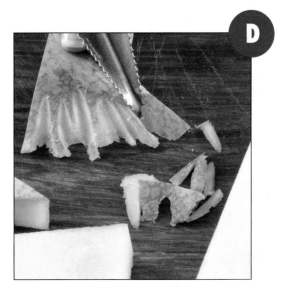

EASTER EGG

Makes 1 basket

Ingredients:
1 honeydew melon
1 wedge cantaloupe
1 wedge watermelon
2 packages (2 ounces each) marshmallow bunnies

For Decorating:
Jelly beans
Easter eggs
Easter grass

Method:
1. Use a large knife to cut the bottom off the honeydew melon so it sits flat (A).
2. Use the **CHANNEL KNIFE** to pull three rows around the honeydew melon (B).
3. Use a knife to trim away the rind around the honeydew melon between the top and center row (C).
4. Use the **DUAL MELON BALLER** to create divots around the honeydew melon.
5. Use the **DUAL FLUTED SCOOP** to create a scalloped opening on top of the honeydew melon (D).
6. Use the **DUAL MELON BALLER** to scoop balls from the cantaloupe and melons.
7. Place melon balls in alternating colors into the divots around the honeydew melon (E).
8. Fill the honeydew melon with melon balls then place on a plate.
9. Skewer melon balls and marshmallow bunnies (F) then add to the honeydew melon.
10. Arrange the jelly beans, eggs and grass around the honeydew melon before serving.

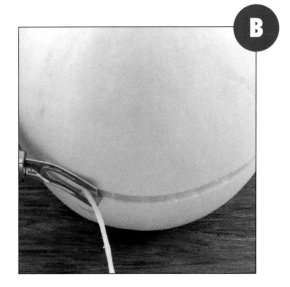

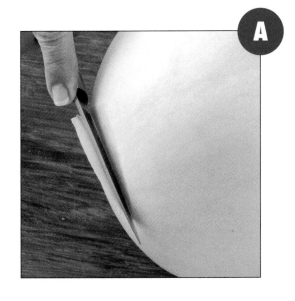

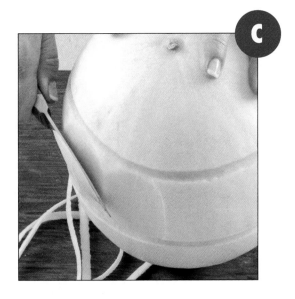

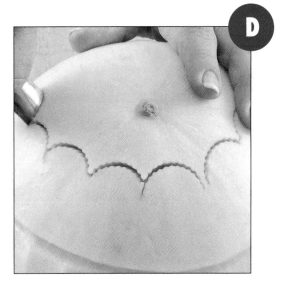

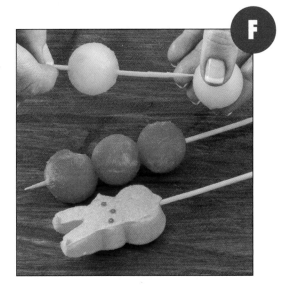

100% FRUIT BIRTHDAY CAKE

Makes 8-10 servings

Ingredients:

1 medium watermelon, seedless
2 kiwi
1/2 of a cantaloupe
1/2 honeydew melon
1 cup blueberries

Method:

1. *Use a large knife to trim the top and bottom from the watermelon so it sits flat and has a flat surface.*
2. *Use the **CRINKLE CUTTER** to trim the sides using a glass bowl as a guide so that the watermelon has round sides (A).*
3. *Use the **Y-PEELER** to peel the kiwi.*
4. *Use the **CRINKLE CUTTER** to slice the kiwi then attach to the sides using pieces of bamboo skewer (B).*
5. *Use the **DUAL MELON BALLER** to scoop balls from the cantaloupe and honeydew then arrange around the base of the watermelon like a border (C).*
6. *Use a flower-shaped cookie cutter to cut a flower out of the honeydew melon and place on top of the watermelon.*
7. *Use the **DUAL MELON BALLER** to scoop a divot out of the center of the flower then add a melon ball (D & E).*
8. *Use a heart-shaped cookie cutter and cut hearts from the cantaloupe then attach to the sides of the watermelon using pieces of bamboo skewer (F).*
9. *Arrange the blueberries around the top edge to form a top border.*
10. *Add birthday candles if desired before serving.*

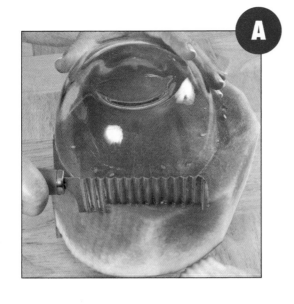

37

OWL BASKET

Makes 4-6 servings

Ingredients:

1 small watermelon
1 wedge cantaloupe
1 wedge honeydew melon
2 store-bought googly eyes

Method:

1. *Use a large knife to cut the bottom off the watermelon so it sits flat (A).*
2. *Use the **DUAL FLUTED SCOOP** to create a fluted opening on one side of the watermelon (B).*
3. *Use the **DUAL MELON BALLER** to scoop balls from the watermelon, cantaloupe and honeydew melon; set aside.*
4. *Use the **CHANNEL KNIFE** to create a "feather" pattern on the owl's tummy on the opposite side of the fluted opening (C).*
5. *Use a knife to cut out wings, feet, eyebrow and beak from the rind of the removed watermelon opening (D).*
6. *Use the **Y-PEELER** to remove the rind from the "eyebrow" (E).*
7. *Secure the nose and eyebrow to the watermelon using small wooden toothpicks (F).*
8. *Affix the googly eyes, place the feet in front of the watermelon then fill body with melon balls.*

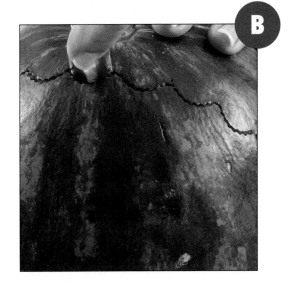

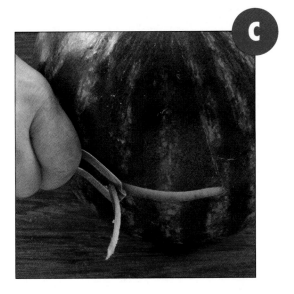

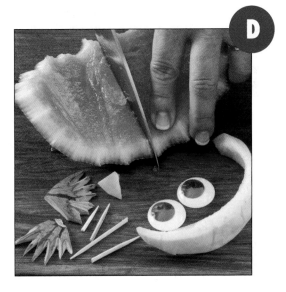

NEW YEAR'S BASKET

Makes 8-10 servings

Ingredients:

1 large watermelon
1 wedge honeydew melon
1 wedge cantaloupe
Store-bought crispy rice treats
4 cups strawberries
1 cup blueberries
2 kiwi
Sparklers

Method:

1. *Use a large knife to cut the bottom off the watermelon so it sits flat (A).*
2. *Trace desired year on a piece of paper; cut out (B) then pin to the side of the watermelon.*
3. *Use a wooden skewer to trace the outline of the pinned year on the watermelon then cut out using a knife (C & D).*
4. *Use the **DUAL FLUTED SCOOP** to create a fluted border around the center of the watermelon.*
5. *Remove the top half of the watermelon.*
6. *Use the **DUAL MELON BALLER** to scoop ball from the melons and cantaloupe then add to the basket.*
7. *Press a star-shaped cookie cutter into the rice treats (E).*
8. *Skewer the strawberries, blueberries and rice treat stars using wooden skewers.*
9. *Use the **CRINKLE CUTTER** to slice the kiwi (F) then add to the basket.*
10. *Arrange the skewers, additional berries and sparklers in the basket.*
11. *Arrange any extra fruit around basket before serving.*

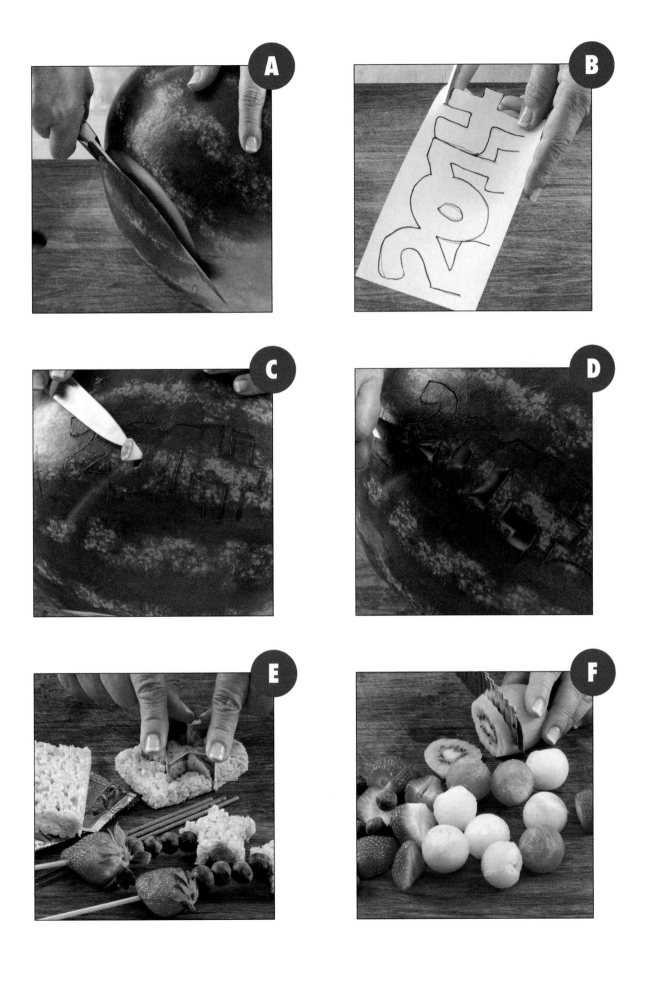

PINEAPPLE DESSERT WEDGES

Makes 4 servings

Ingredients:

1 large ripe pineapple
1 lime
3 tablespoons sugar
1 piece fresh coconut
A few sprigs fresh mint

Method:

1. *Use a large knife to quarter the pineapple lengthwise, leaving the crown on (A).*
2. *Use a knife to separate the flesh from the rind (B).*
3. *Use a knife to remove the core.*
4. *Use a knife to carve 2 decorative notches down the length of each side (C).*
5. *Use the **CRINKLE CUTTER** to slice each wedge vertically to create individual slices (D).*
6. *Use the **CITRUS ZESTER** to zest the lime into a small bowl.*
7. *Use a knife to cut lime in half then squeeze the juice over the zest and stir in the sugar.*
8. *Drizzle sugar mixture over the pineapple wedges.*
9. *Place on individual plates then grate coconut over the pineapple using the **MEDIUM GRATER**.*
10. *Use the **HERB SHEARS** to snip some mint for garnish before serving.*

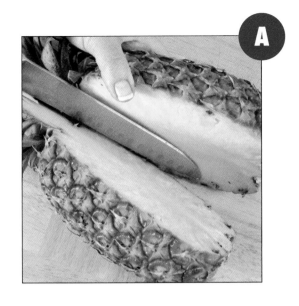

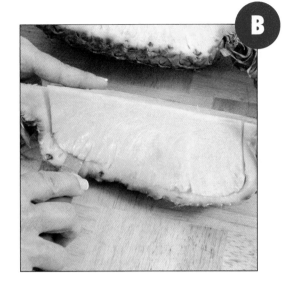

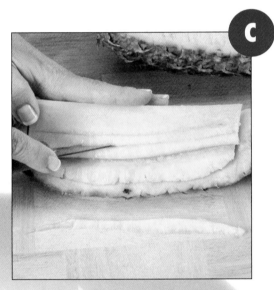

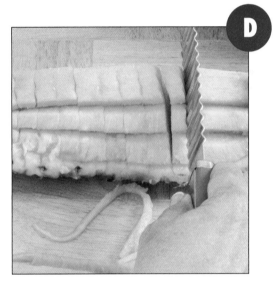

PIGGY BASKET

Makes 5-6 servings

Ingredients:

1 honeydew melon
1 wedge watermelon
1 wedge cantaloupe
1 pink pipe cleaner
2 store-bought googly eyes

Method:

1. *Use a large knife to cut an opening into the honeydew melon then remove the top (A).*
2. *Use the **DUAL MELON BALLER** to scoop balls from the melons and cantaloupe; set aside.*
3. *Use a knife to trim a piece of watermelon rind into a round snout using a ramekin as a guide (B).*
4. *Use a knife to trim feet, mouth and ears from additional watermelon rind (C).*
5. *Use the **V-SLICER** to cut nostrils into the snout (D).*
6. *Wrap the pink pipe cleaner around the handle of a wooden spoon to coil it (E).*
7. *Affix the googly eyes to the pig's face then use wooden toothpicks to secure the ears, mouth, snout and feet to the melon (F).*
8. *Attach the tail then fill the basket with melon balls.*

44

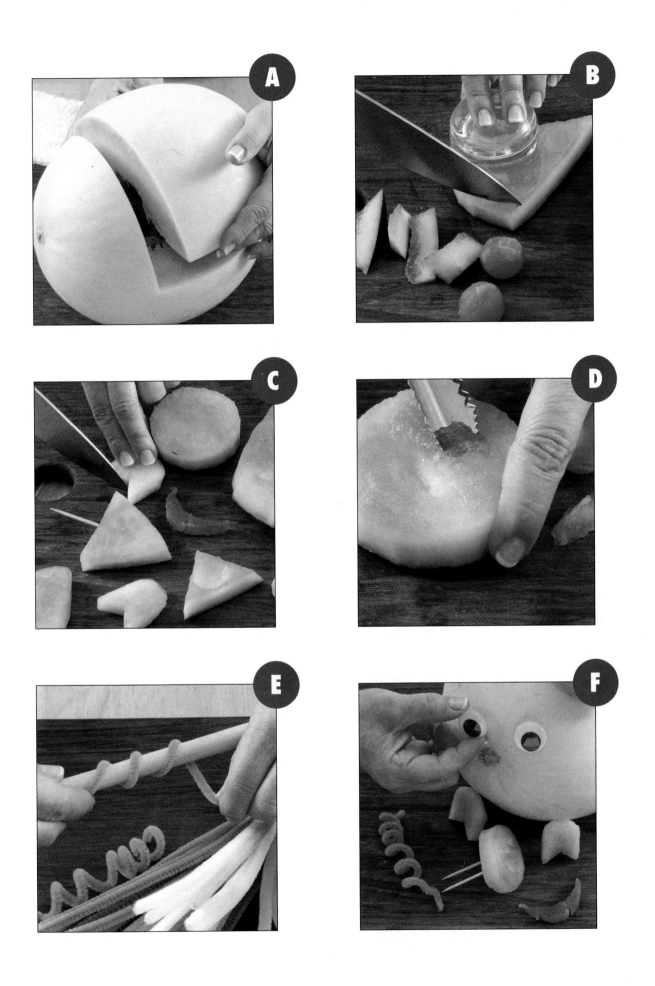

45

MELON SHARK

Makes 8-10 servings

Ingredients:

1 large watermelon
2 black olives
1 cup fish-shaped wine gum candy

Method:

1. *Use a knife to cut the bottom off the watermelon at an angle so the shark looks like it is coming out of the water (A).*
2. *Use a knife to cut out a large wedge for the mouth (B).*
3. *Use the **CRINKLE CUTTER** to cut the flesh from the watermelon wedge into chunks.*
4. *Use the **V-SLICER** to create teeth on either side of the mouth (C).*
5. *Use the **DUAL MELON BALLER** to scoop out eye sockets or use a knife if the flesh is too tough (D).*
6. *Use a wooden toothpick to attach a black olive to each eye socket (E).*
7. *Use the **CHANNEL KNIFE** to pull gills on both sides of the watermelon (F).*
8. *Cut a dorsal fin from watermelon rind then attach using wooden toothpicks.*
9. *Place on platter with watermelon chunks and candy.*

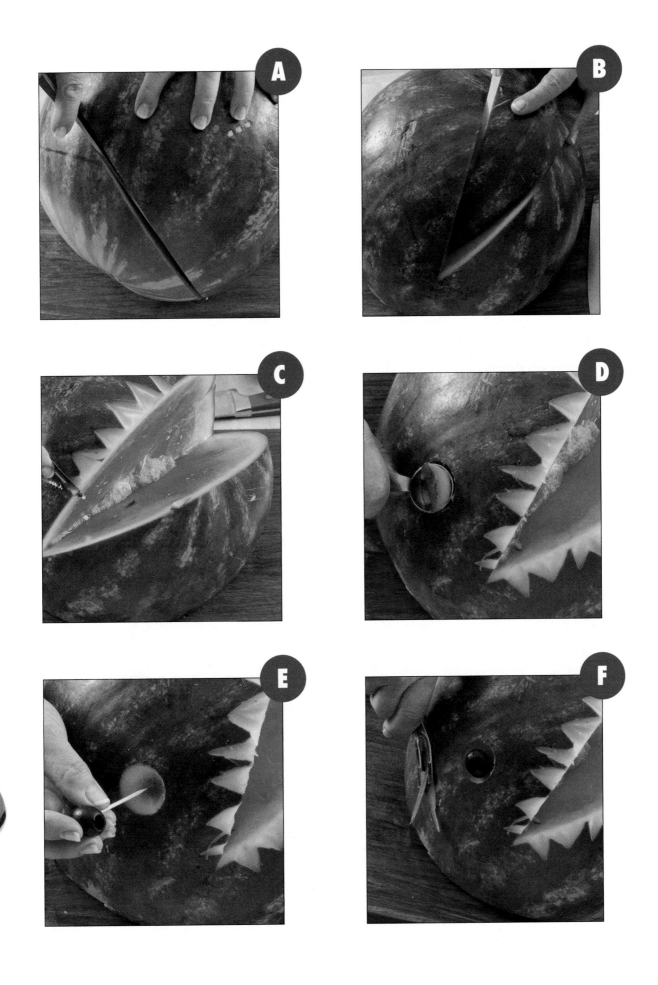

THANKSGIVING TURKEY RELISH PLATTER

Makes 8-10 servings

Ingredients:

4 hard boiled eggs
5 small tomatoes
1 leek
4 cups baby carrots
1 green bell pepper
1 red bell pepper
1 yellow bell pepper
5 large collard greens

Method:

1. Use the **WIRE SLICER** to slice the eggs using the non-serrated side of the slicer (A).
2. Use the **WIRE SLICER** to slice the tomatoes using the serrated side of the slicer (B).
3. Use the **CRINKLE CUTTER** to slice the leek into 3-inch pieces (C).
4. Use the **HERB SHEARS** to frill the leek pieces, then cut into fourths to create legs (D).
5. Use the **APPLE CORER** to cut eye sockets from egg white slices (E).
6. Use a knife to cut pieces of baby carrots for the eyeballs.
7. Use the **CRINKLE CUTTER** to make the "face" by cutting off the bottom of the green bell pepper (F).
8. Use the **CRINKLE CUTTER** to slice remaining bell peppers into half rings.
9. Cut out the snood and beak from bell pepper scraps.
10. Arrange the food to make a turkey according to the photo.

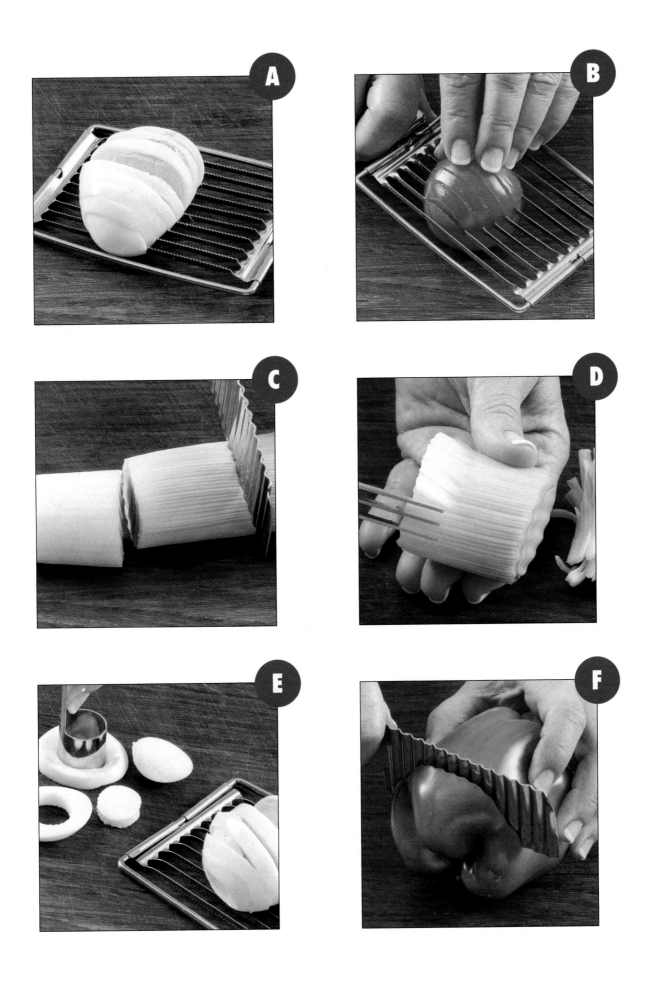

WATERMELON WEDGE CAKE

Makes 8 servings

Ingredients:

1 large watermelon
A few mint sprigs

Method:

1. *Use a large knife to cut the top third off the watermelon (A).*
2. *Make another cut 3-inches away from the first cut to cut off the other end of the watermelon (B), leaving you with a thick and round center melon piece.*
3. *Use a knife to cut the round center piece in half (C).*
4. *Cut the round center piece into 8 equal wedges (D) then place on a serving platter.*
5. *Use the **DUAL MELON BALLER** to scoop melon balls from the removed watermelon top and bottom then arrange melon balls neatly across the top of the "cake" (E).*
6. *Garnish with mint sprigs before serving (F).*

50

BIRTHDAY FRUIT BOWL

Makes 12-15 servings

Ingredients:

1 large watermelon, seedless
1 honeydew melon
1 cantaloupe
1 pint raspberries
1 pint blueberries
1 pint strawberries
3 cups chocolate chips
1/2 cup coconut oil
Large marshmallows

Method:

1. *Use a large knife to cut the bottom off the watermelon so it sits flat.*
2. *Use the **V-SLICER** to cut a large opening into the top of the watermelon; reserve usable flesh (A).*
3. *To add a name or message to the watermelon, trace letters into the rind of the watermelon using a bamboo skewer (B).*
4. *Use a knife to remove the flesh around the letters (C).*
5. *Use the **DUAL MELON BALLER** to scoop balls from the melons and cantaloupe (D).*
6. *Transfer the melon balls to the watermelon basket then add the raspberries, blueberries and some strawberries; arrange some extra melon balls around the watermelon if desired.*
7. *In a microwave-safe bowl, combine the chocolate chips and coconut oil.*
8. *Microwave for 1 minute then stir and repeat until chocolate is fluid.*
9. *Place marshmallows and strawberries on long bamboo skewers then dip into the fluid chocolate before placing them in the fruit basket.*
10. *Add long birthday candles if desired before serving.*

52

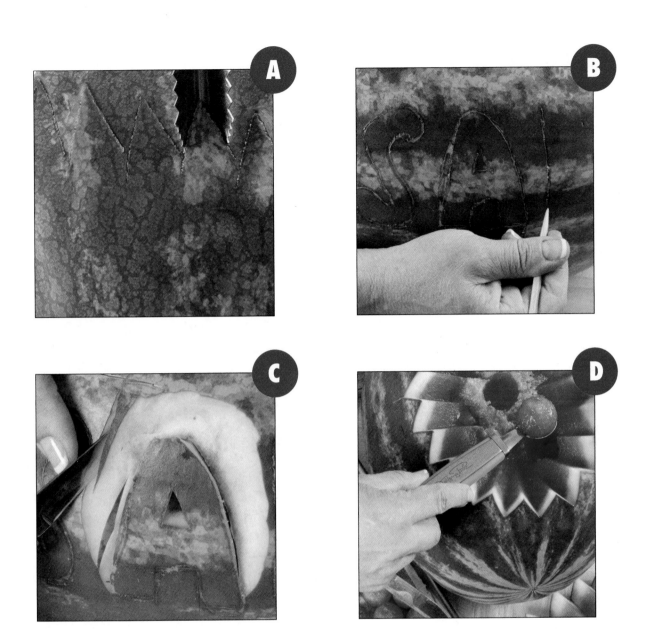

TORNADO POTATO

Makes 8 servings

Ingredients:

8 Yukon Gold potatoes
Oil for frying
Kosher salt

Method:

1. *Insert the screw part of the **SPIRAL SLICER** into one end of a potato (A).*
2. *Press in the screw firmly while turning the potato until it is flush with the potato (B).*
3. *Insert your finger into the ring of the **SPIRAL SLICER** and hold steady (C).*
4. *Turn the potato against the blade.*
5. *Continue slicing until half of the potato is sliced then break off the potato (D).*
6. *Rinse under cold water then pat dry using paper towels.*
7. *Insert a long bamboo skewer through the bottom of the potato (not the same hole where you inserted the screw or it will fall off the skewer) then ruffle open (E & F).*
8. *Repeat with additional potatoes.*
9. *Fry in oil at 350°F for 8 minutes or until well browned; turn once during frying.*
10. *Remove and drain on paper towels; salt immediately.*
11. *Stand chips upright using a potato half as a base and let cool before serving.*

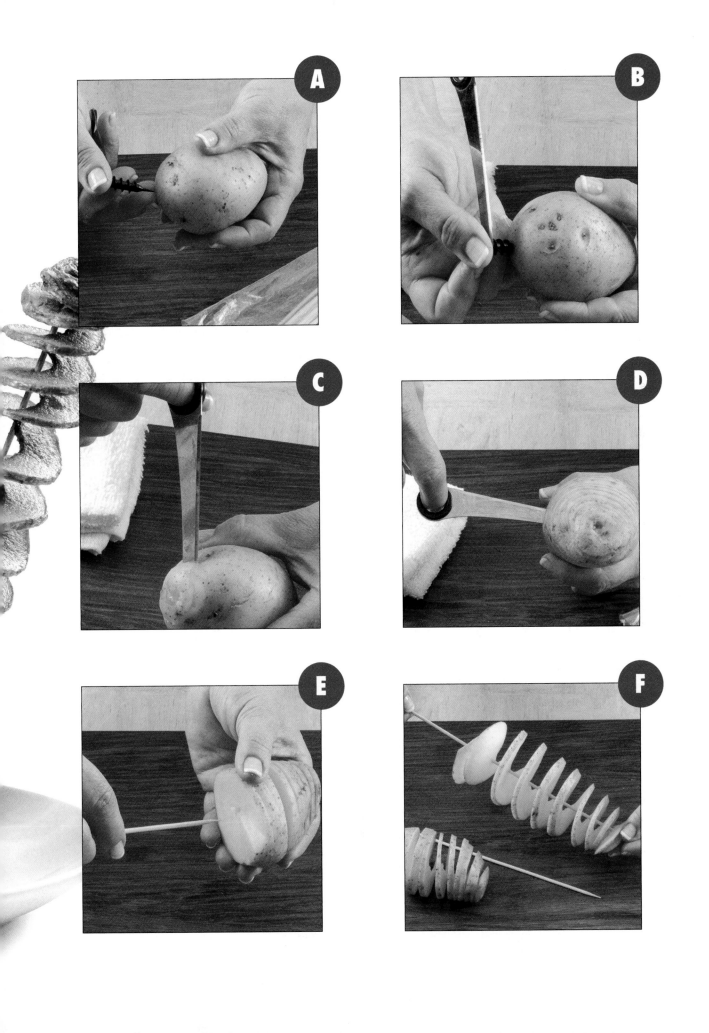

SMILEY FACE

Makes 4-6 servings

Ingredients:

1 small watermelon
1 wedge cantaloupe
1 wedge honeydew melon
1 wedge pineapple
1 cup red grapes

Method:

1. *Use a large knife to cut the bottom off the watermelon so it sits flat (A).*
2. *Trace the eyes and mouth on a piece of paper; cut out (B) then pin to the watermelon.*
3. *Use a wooden skewer to trace the outline of the pinned eyes and mouth onto the watermelon then cut out using a knife (C).*
4. *Use flower-shaped cookie cutters to make some flowers from cantaloupe, honeydew melon and pineapple (D).*
5. *Use the **DUAL FLUTED SCOOP** to make a fluted opening into the top of the watermelon.*
6. *Use the **APPLE CORER** to make watermelon flower centers from watermelon flesh (E).*
7. *Use the **DUAL MELON BALLER** to scoop balls from remaining cantaloupe and melon flesh (F).*
8. *Secure flowers and centers to the side of the watermelon using wooden toothpicks.*
9. *Fill smiley face with melon balls and grapes.*

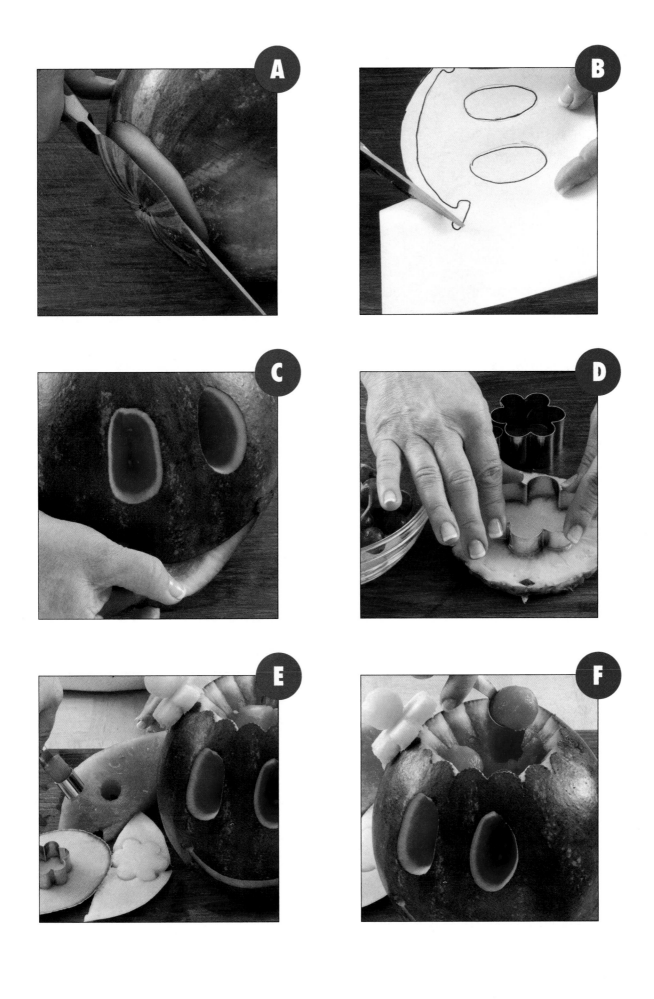

100% PINEAPPLE BIRTHDAY CAKE

Makes 4-6 servings

Ingredients:

1 pineapple
1 wedge honeydew melon
1 wedge cantaloupe
1 wedge watermelon
1 kiwi

Method:

1. Use the **CRINKLE CUTTER** to trim the pineapple then remove the rind (A).
2. Use the **APPLE CORER** to remove the pineapple core (B).
3. Use the **DUAL MELON BALLER** to scoop balls from the honeydew melon.
4. Use a heart-shaped cookie cutter to cut out melon hearts from the cantaloupe wedge (C).
5. Use the **CRINKLE CUTTER** to slice the kiwi then use a flower-shaped cookie cutter to cut out kiwi flowers (D).
6. Use the fluted end of the **DUAL MELON BALLER** to scoop balls from the watermelon wedge (E).
7. Arrange the honeydew and watermelon balls as top and bottom borders (F).
8. Secure the melon hearts and flowers to the side of the pineapple using wooden toothpicks.
9. Add a honeydew ball and candle to the top before serving.

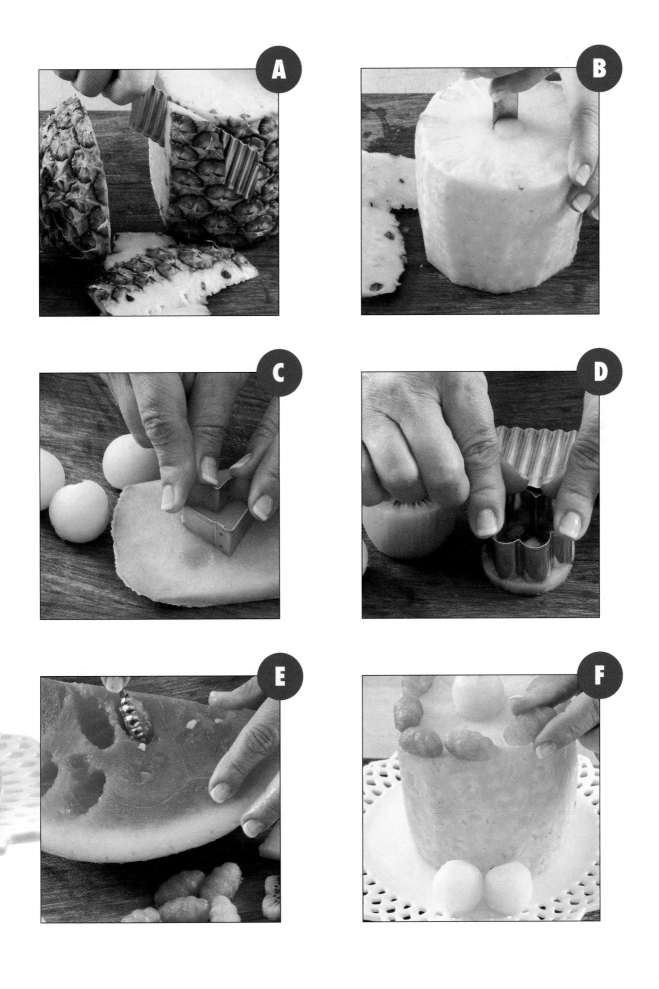

HOW OLD ARE YOU?

Makes 5-6 servings

Ingredients:

1 small watermelon
1 wedge honeydew melon
1 wedge cantaloupe
1 cup white chocolate chips
Food coloring
6 large marshmallows
Sprinkles
Candles (optional)

Method:

1. *Use a large knife to cut the bottom off the watermelon so it sits flat.*
2. *Trace desired number on a piece of paper; cut out (A) then pin to the side of the watermelon.*
3. *Use a wooden skewer to trace the outline of the pinned number on the watermelon then cut out using a knife (B).*
4. *Use the **DUAL FLUTED SCOOP** to create a fluted border around the center of the watermelon (C).*
5. *Remove the top half of the watermelon (D).*
6. *Use the **DUAL MELON BALLER** to scoop balls from the melons and cantaloupe then add to the basket (E).*
7. *Microwave the chocolate chips for 1-3 minutes or until melted then add desired food coloring.*
8. *Skewer the marshmallows onto straws then dip into chocolates as desired (F).*
9. *Dip chocolate covered marshmallows in sprinkles then add to basket with candles if desired.*

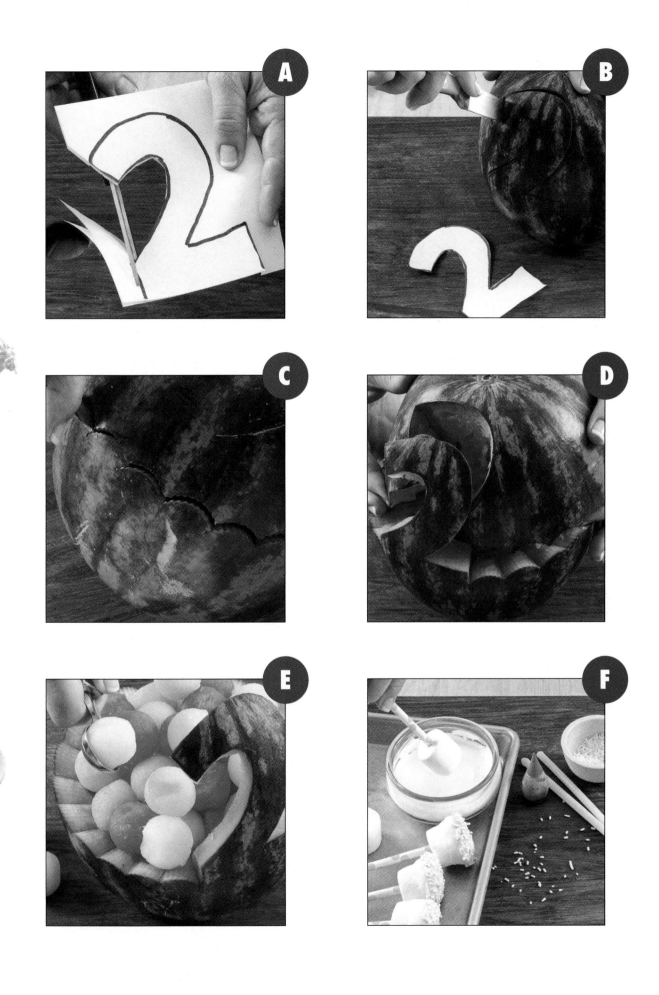

WORMS IN DIRT
JACK-O-LANTERN

Makes 1 Jack-O-Lantern

Ingredients:

1 butternut squash
1 glow stick
1 cup chocolate cookie crumbs
24 gummy worms

Method:

1. *Use a knife to cut the bottom off the butternut squash so it sits flat (A) then use a spoon to hollow out the squash's bottom.*
2. *Use a knife to cut off the top from the squash (B); reserve top.*
3. *Use the **DUAL MELON BALLER** to hollow out the squash's neck (C).*
4. *Use the **APPLE CORER** to poke random holes into the sides of the squash (D).*
5. *Drop an activated glow stick into the neck of the squash (E) then replace top.*
6. *Place the squash on a plate then scatter cookie crumb "dirt" around it.*
7. *Place worms into the holes and dirt before serving (F).*

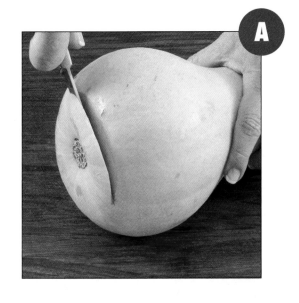

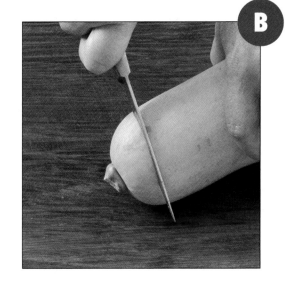

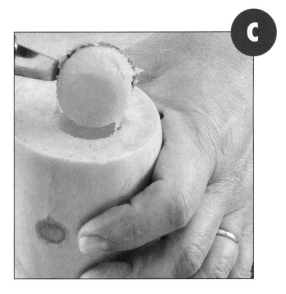

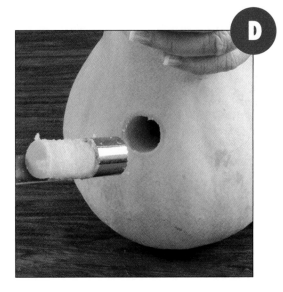

THANKSGIVING FRUIT BASKET

Makes 12-15 servings

Ingredients:

1 large watermelon, seedless
1 honeydew melon
1 cantaloupe
3 kiwi
1 package fresh blueberries
1/3 cup granulated sugar
1/4 cup apple juice
1 teaspoon lemon juice
1/2 teaspoon vanilla extract

Method:

1. *Use a large knife to cut the bottom off the watermelon so it sits flat (A).*
2. *Draw a turkey on a piece paper to make a template; cut it out using scissors.*
3. *Attach the turkey template to the side of the watermelon using tape.*
4. *Trace the turkey outline on the side of the watermelon using a bamboo skewer (B) then deepen the lines using a knife (C).*
5. *Use a knife to remove the flesh around the turkey shape (D).*
6. *Use the V-SLICER to cut an oval opening into the top of the watermelon; reserve usable flesh (E).*
7. *Use the DUAL MELON BALLER to scoop balls from the melons and cantaloupe (F).*
8. *Use the Y-PEELER to peel the kiwi then slice them using the CRINKLE CUTTER.*
9. *Use a maple leaf-shaped cookie cutter to cut out shapes from the melons then place on long bamboo skewers.*
10. *Fill the basket with melon balls, kiwi and blueberries then add the skewered maple leaves.*
11. *In a small bowl, stir together remaining ingredients.*
12. *Pour mixture into a spray bottle then spray the fruit before serving.*

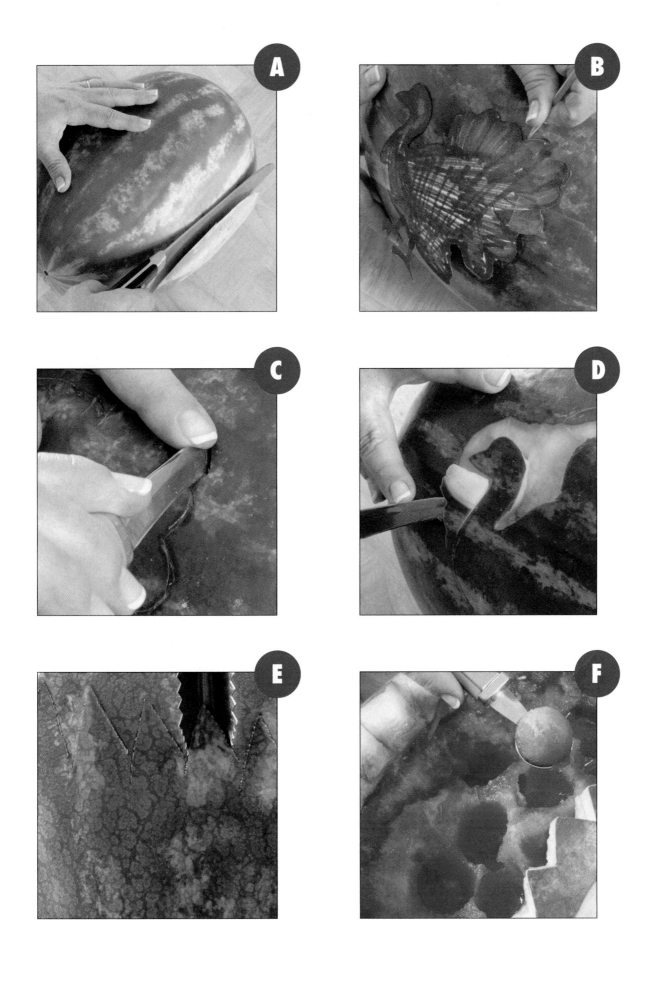

100% FRUIT
WEDDING CAKE

Makes 10-15 servings

Ingredients:

2 medium watermelons, seedless
2 pints blueberries

Method:

1. *Use a large knife to cut both watermelons in half vertically.*
2. *Use a large knife to trim off all the rind from the watermelons (A).*
3. *Cut a 4-inch thick bottom tier from 1 watermelon half by using a glass bowl as a guide so that the watermelon tier has round sides (B).*
4. *Use the **CRINKLE CUTTER** to trim another 4-inch thick tier; use a smaller glass bowl as a guide to cut this tier 2 inches less in diameter than the first one (C).*
5. *Use a knife to trim another 4-inch thick tier; use a smaller coffee cup as a guide to cut this tier 2 inches less in diameter than the second tier (D).*
6. *Place the first tier on a cake pedestal then top with the second and third tier.*
7. *Arrange the blueberries around each tier like a border (E).*
8. *Use a small heart-shaped cookie cutter to cut a heart from the remaining watermelon.*
9. *Place heart on a long bamboo skewer then push into the top tier before serving (F).*

ST. PATRICK'S DAY FRUIT BASKET

Makes 6-8 servings

Ingredients:
1 honeydew melon
1 cantaloupe
3 kiwi
1 bunch green grapes
1/3 cup granulated sugar
1/4 cup apple juice
1 teaspoon lemon juice
1/2 teaspoon vanilla extract

Method:
1. *Use a large knife to cut the bottom off the honeydew melon so it sits flat.*
2. *Use a shamrock-shaped cookie cutter and a meat mallet to tap shamrocks onto the side of the melon (A).*
3. *Use a knife to remove the flesh around the shamrocks (B).*
4. *Use the **V-SLICER** to cut a round opening into the top of the honeydew melon; reserve usable flesh.*
5. *Use the **DUAL MELON BALLER** to scoop balls from the honeydew melon and cantaloupe.*
6. *Use the **Y-PEELER** to peel the kiwi then slice them using the **CRINKLE CUTTER**.*
7. *Use the shamrock-shaped cookie cutter to cut out shapes from the melons then place on long bamboo skewers.*
8. *Fill the basket with melon balls, grapes and kiwi then add the skewered shamrocks.*
9. *In a small bowl, stir together remaining ingredients.*
10. *Pour mixture into a spray bottle then spray the fruit before serving.*

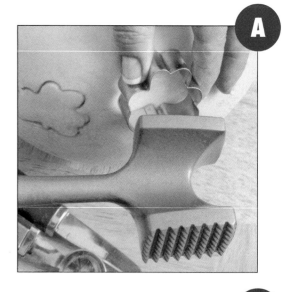

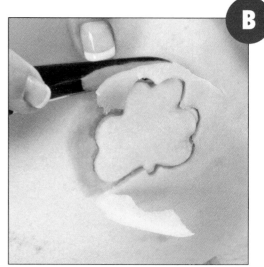

PRETTY PINEAPPLE BOATS

Makes 4 servings

Ingredients:

1 ripe pineapple with crown
1/2 honeydew melon
1 kiwi
1/4 cup granulated sugar
1/4 cup water
1 teaspoon lemon juice
1/4 teaspoon vanilla extract

Method:

1. Use the **CRINKLE CUTTER** to trim the pineapple crown (A).
2. Use the **V-SLICER** to cut around the pineapple at a 45° angle.
3. Remove the pineapple flesh using a knife, leaving a 1/2-inch thick shell (B).
4. Rinse out the pineapple shell if any of the brown rind remains.
5. Use the **DUAL MELON BALLER** to scoop balls from the honeydew melon.
6. Fill the boat with honeydew balls.
7. Use the **V-SLICER** to cut kiwi in half then place around the pineapple (C).
8. In a bowl whisk together the sugar, water, lemon and vanilla.
9. Drizzle sugar mixture over the fruit before serving.

VALENTINE'S DAY
FRUIT BASKET

Makes 4-6 servings

Ingredients:

1 watermelon, seedless
1 honeydew melon
1 cantaloupe
1/3 cup granulated sugar
1/4 cup apple juice
1 teaspoon lemon juice
1/2 teaspoon vanilla extract

Method:

1. *Use a large knife to cut the bottom off the watermelon so it sits flat.*
2. *Use a heart-shaped cookie cutter and a mallet to tap hearts into the side of the watermelon, making sure to go through the rind of the watermelon (A).*
3. *Use a knife to remove the flesh around the heart shapes (B).*
4. *Use the **V-SLICER** to cut an oval opening into the top of the watermelon; reserve usable flesh (C).*
5. *Use the **DUAL MELON BALLER** to scoop balls from the melons and cantaloupe.*
6. *Use the heart-shaped cookie cutters to cut out shapes from the melons then place on long bamboo skewers (D).*
7. *Fill the basket with melon balls then add the skewered hearts.*
8. *In a small bowl, stir together remaining ingredients.*
9. *Pour mixture into a spray bottle then spray the fruit before serving.*

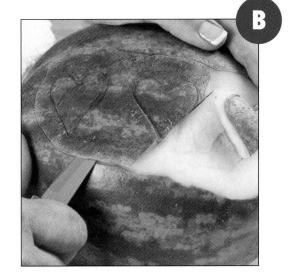

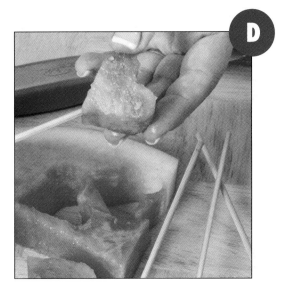

HONEYDEW MELON
FLOWER

Makes 4-6 servings

Ingredients:

1 honeydew melon
1 watermelon wedge, seedless

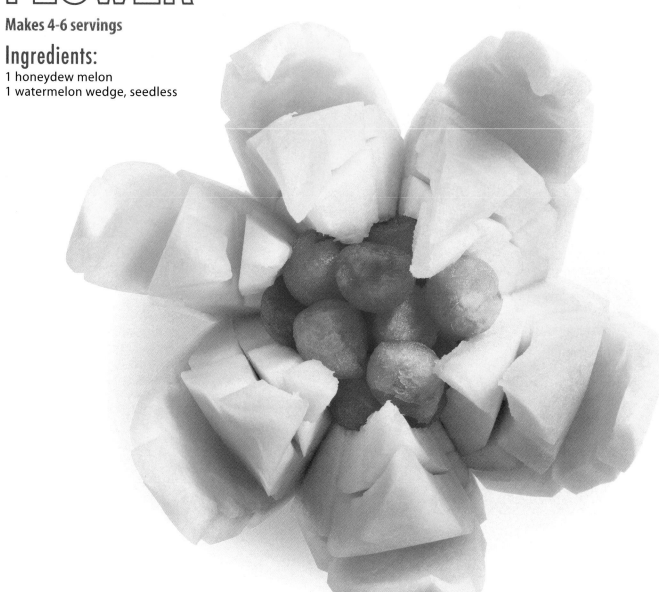

Method:

1. Use a large knife to cut the bottom off the honeydew melon so it sits flat.
2. Use a knife to cut out v-shaped flower petals from the honeydew melon (A) then remove the top half (B).
3. Use a knife to cut notches into each petal (C).
4. Use a knife to cut down each of the petals twice to separate the flesh from the rind and to open up the petals (D & E).
5. Use the **DUAL MELON BALLER** to scoop balls from the watermelon wedge.
6. Gather up the balls then place them in the center of the honeydew flower (F).
7. Garnish as desired and serve.

GRADUATION FRUIT BASKET

Makes 10-15 servings

Ingredients:

1 large watermelon, seedless
1 honeydew melon
1 cantaloupe
1 pineapple
1 pint blueberries
1 bunch green grapes
1 pint strawberries
2 cups chocolate chips
1 cup white chocolate chips
1/3 cup coconut oil

FRUIT DISPLAYS

Method:

1. Use a large knife to cut the bottom off the watermelon so it sits flat.
2. Use the **V-SLICER** to cut an opening into the top of the watermelon; reserve lid (A).
3. Use the **APPLE CORER** to punch a hole border around the watermelon (B).
4. Use a large knife to slice the rind off one side of the watermelon (C).
5. Using alphabet cookie cutters, cut desired letters from the watermelon flesh of the removed lid then attach to the side of the watermelon using small pieces of bamboo skewer (D).
6. Use the **DUAL MELON BALLER** to scoop balls from the melons and cantaloupe.
7. Use a knife to trim and peel the pineapple.
8. Use the **APPLE CORER** to remove the pineapple core then cut pineapple into pieces using the **CRINKLE CUTTER**.
9. Fill the basket with melon balls, pineapple, blueberries and grapes.
10. Place the strawberries on long bamboo skewers.
11. Place each color chocolate chips into a separate microwave-safe bowl.
12. Divide the coconut oil between the bowls then microwave each for 30 seconds.
13. Stir and repeat until fluid.
14. Dip skewered strawberries into either color chocolate then drizzle with other chocolate to make a pretty design if desired before adding to the basket (E).

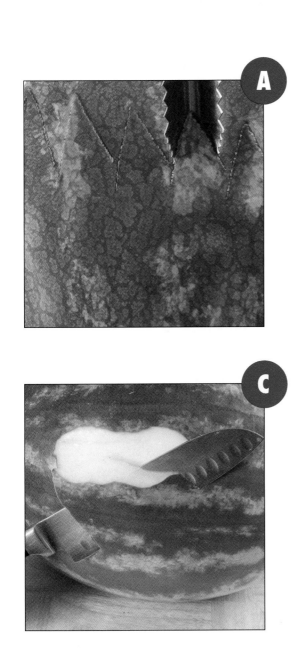

A

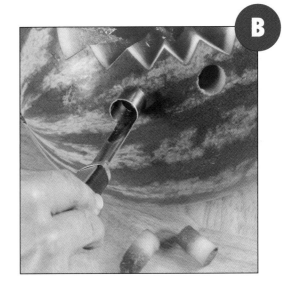

B

C

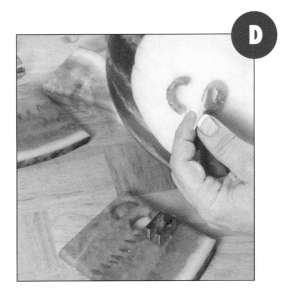

D

E

PAPER FRILL BOOTIES

Makes 2 booties

Component:
2 sheets white paper

Method:
1. *Fold 1 sheet of paper in half lengthwise.*
2. *Use the **HERB SHEARS** to snip 1-inch deep on the folded edge (A).*
3. *Continue snipping along the length of the entire paper (B).*
4. *Pull open the paper (C) then fold in the opposite direction (D) until the fold is reversed without creasing the cut end.*
5. *Fold up excess paper until it touches the beginning of the frilled part (E).*
6. *Roll up as wide as the drumstick end of your poultry then secure the end using clear tape (F).*
7. *Repeat with remaining piece of paper.*
8. *Slide over the end of each drumstick before serving.*

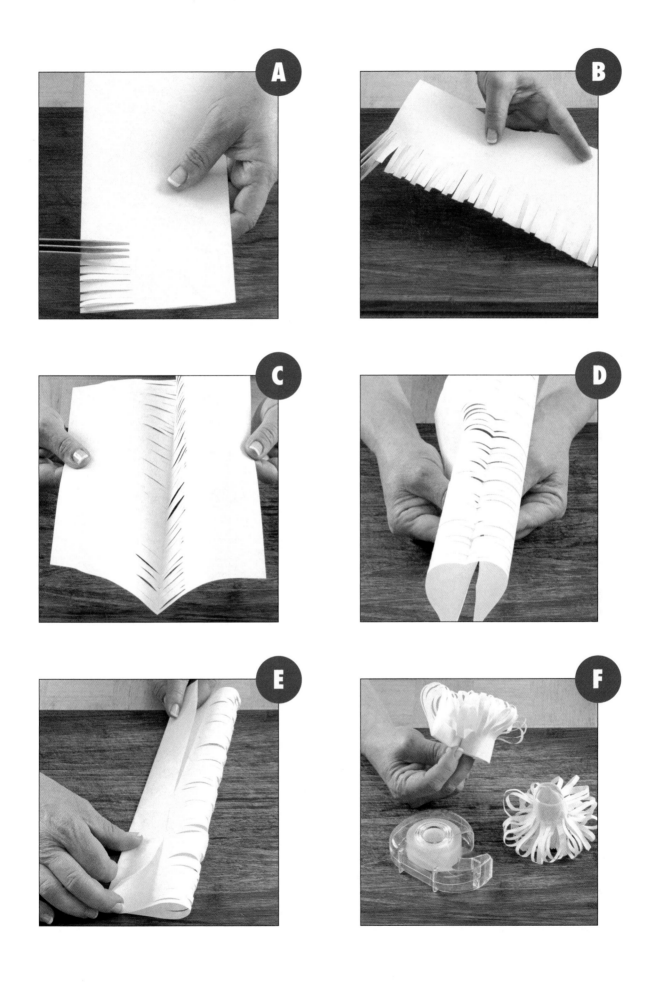

CHEESEBURGER PIZZA

Makes 1 pizza

Ingredients:

1 tablespoon canola oil
1 pound ground beef
Kosher salt and fresh pepper to taste
1 medium yellow onion
1 pound pizza dough, store-bought
1/2 cup ketchup
1/4 cup yellow mustard
2 dill pickles
1 small wedge Cheddar cheese

Method:

1. Preheat oven to 450°F.
2. Preheat the oil in a large sauté pan over medium-high heat.
3. When pan is hot, add the ground beef; seasoning with salt and pepper.
4. Use the **MEDIUM GRATER** to grate the onion over the ground beef in the pan; stir.
5. When meat is browned, remove and drain.
6. Pat out the pizza dough on a greased jelly roll pan.
7. In a small bowl, stir together the ketchup and mustard.
8. Spread the ketchup mixture over the dough then top with the ground beef mixture.
9. Use the **Y-PEELER** to thinly shave the pickles; scatter over the pizza.
10. Use the **MEDIUM GRATER** to shred the cheese over the pizza until evenly covered.
11. Bake for 20 minutes or until browned and bubbly then remove and let stand for 5 minutes.
12. Cut pizza into slices and serve.

MEXICAN BEEF CASSEROLE

Makes 4-6 servings

For the Casserole:

1 large yellow onion
1 jalapeño pepper
1 tablespoon canola oil
1 pound ground beef
1 can (15.5 ounces) kidney beans, drained and rinsed
1 can (15.5 ounces) yellow corn
1 jar (17.35 ounces) enchilada sauce
1 can (4 ounces) diced green chiles
1 package (1.12 ounces) taco seasoning mix
2 cups beef stock

For Serving:

4 cups tortilla chips
1 cup Monterrey Jack cheese
Jalapeño peppers
Sour cream
Green onions

Method:

1. Preheat oven to 350°F.
2. Use the **CRINKLE CUTTER** to chop the onion and jalapeño pepper.
3. Preheat the oil in a large skillet over medium-high heat.
4. When oil is hot, add the beef; cook and stir until no longer pink then transfer to a 9 x 13-inch baking dish.
5. Add remaining casserole ingredients to the baking dish; stir well.
6. Bake for 30-40 minutes or until brown and bubbly.
7. Add the tortilla chips to the casserole.
8. Use the **MEDIUM GRATER** to shred the cheese over the casserole then serve as desired.

EASY GLAZED MEATLOAF

Makes 4-6 servings

For the Meatloaf:

1 large yellow onion
4 bacon slices
1/2 cup breadcrumbs
1/3 cup whole milk
2 garlic cloves, minced
1 pound lean ground beef
1/2 pound ground pork
2 large eggs, beaten
1 teaspoon kosher salt
1/2 teaspoon freshly cracked pepper
1/3 cup ketchup
1 tablespoon yellow mustard
1 tablespoon Worcestershire sauce
Parsley for garnish

For the Glaze:

1/4 cup yellow mustard
1/3 cup ketchup
1 cup light brown sugar, packed

Method:

1. Preheat oven to 350°F.
2. Use the **CRINKLE CUTTER** to finely chop the onion and bacon.
3. In a bowl, combine the breadcrumbs and milk; let stand for 5 minutes.
4. Add remaining meatloaf ingredients, except parsley, to the bowl; mix gently together.
5. Apply nonstick spray to a baking pan or bread pan.
6. Press the meatloaf mixture into the pan then smooth the top; cover with aluminum foil.
7. Place pan in oven and bake for 1 hour.
8. Combine all glaze ingredients in a saucepan over medium heat.
9. Simmer for 5 minutes or until thick and shiny.
10. When baking is complete, remove meatloaf from the oven and top with glaze.
11. Use the **HERB SHEARS** to cut parsley over the meatloaf before serving.

BBQ BEEF BRISKET DINNER

Makes 6-8 servings

Ingredients:

2 large carrots
2 celery stalks
2 large yellow onions, quartered
3 pounds beef brisket, trimmed
1 tablespoon beef bouillon powder, such as Maggi
1 1/2 cups ginger ale or water
1/2 cup ketchup
1 cup bottled BBQ sauce
Kosher salt and fresh black pepper to taste

Method:

1. *Preheat oven to 300°F.*
2. *Use the **Y-PEELER** to peel the carrots.*
3. *Use the **CRINKLE CUTTER** to chop the carrots, celery and onions then transfer to a large Dutch oven.*
4. *Layer remaining ingredients in the Dutch oven in the order listed; cover with lid.*
5. *Bake for 4 hours or until meat is tender.*
6. *When baking is complete, garnish as desired before serving.*

BEEF & NOODLES

Makes 4-6 servings

Ingredients:

1/2 medium yellow onion
2 celery stalks
4 ounces button mushrooms
2 garlic cloves
1 tablespoon unsalted butter
1 pound ground beef
1/2 cup chicken stock
1 cup evaporated milk
Kosher salt and fresh pepper to taste
Green onions for garnish
Hot buttered noodles, cooked
Sour cream (optional)

Method:

1. *Preheat a sauté pan over medium-high heat.*
2. *Use the **CRINKLE CUTTER** to chop the onion, celery, mushrooms and garlic; set aside.*
3. *Melt the butter in the pan.*
4. *Add the ground beef to the pan; stir and cook until no pink remains.*
5. *Add the onions, celery, mushrooms and garlic to the pan; cook for 3 minutes or until onions are tender.*
6. *Add remaining ingredients, except green onions, noodles and sour cream; cover with lid.*
7. *Cook for 10-12 minutes then taste and adjust seasoning if desired.*
8. *Use the **HERB SHEARS** to snip the green onions for garnishing.*
9. *Serve over buttered noodles garnished with a dollop of sour cream if desired and green onions.*

EASY ONE SKILLET
BEEF STROGANOFF

Makes 4 servings

Ingredients:

1 1/2 pounds sirloin beef
Kosher salt and fresh pepper to taste
2 tablespoons olive oil
2 large yellow onions
2 garlic cloves
2 packages (10 ounces) button mushrooms
3 cups beef stock
2 teaspoons soy sauce
3 tablespoons brandy or Madeira
3 cups dry egg noodles
2/3 cup sour cream
Fresh parsley

Method:

1. *Slice the beef into thin strips then season with salt and pepper.*
2. *Preheat the oil in a large skillet over medium-high heat.*
3. *When oil is hot, add the beef to the skillet; sear on all sides.*
4. *While meat is searing, slice the onions using the **CRINKLE CUTTER** and add to the skillet.*
5. *Use the **CRINKLE CUTTER** to smash and chop the garlic then transfer to the skillet.*
6. *Use the **CRINKLE CUTTER** to slice the mushrooms then add to the skillet.*
7. *Add the stock and soy sauce to the skillet; stir thoroughly, scraping the bottom of the skillet.*
8. *Add the brandy to the skillet; cover then reduce heat to a simmer.*
9. *Cook for 20 minutes or just until beef is almost tender.*
10. *Stir in the noodles, cover then cook for an additional 8 minutes.*
11. *When cooking is complete, remove from heat then stir in the sour cream.*
12. *Use the **HERB SHEARS** to snip parsley over the dish, garnish as desired and serve.*

BAKED SPAGHETTI

Makes 4-6 servings

Ingredients:

2 teaspoons olive oil
1 pound Italian sausage
1 large yellow onion
6 garlic cloves
2 teaspoons Italian seasoning
1 can (28 ounces) diced tomatoes
Kosher salt and fresh pepper to taste
2 cups hot beef stock
8 ounces dried spaghetti, broken
A small wedge of Parmesan cheese
2-ounce block mozzarella cheese
Fresh basil leaves
Fresh chives

Method:

1. *Preheat the oil in a large skillet over medium-high heat.*
2. *Use the **CRINKLE CUTTER** to roughly chop the Italian sausage, onion and garlic then transfer to the skillet.*
3. *When sausage is no longer pink, add the Italian seasoning, tomatoes, salt and pepper; stir.*
4. *Add the hot stock and spaghetti; cover then turn heat to medium-low and cook for 6 minutes.*
5. *Remove the lid, stir, then cover again and cook for an additional 6 minutes.*
6. *Stir, test noodles for doneness and remove from heat when done.*
7. *Use the **MEDIUM GRATER** to grate both cheeses over the spaghetti.*
8. *If desired, place under the broiler for 2-3 minutes or until lightly browned.*
9. *Use the **HERB SHEARS** to snip basil and chives over the spaghetti before serving.*

CHILI CON CARNE

Makes 4-6 servings

Ingredients:

1 large white onion
6 garlic cloves
1/4 cup green onions
2 pounds beef brisket, trimmed
4 bacon slices
4 tablespoons chili powder
1 tablespoon ground cumin seeds
1 tablespoon oregano leaves
Kosher salt and fresh pepper to taste
4 cups water
2 cups canned tomato puree
1 teaspoon honey
Juice from 1 lime
1 jalapeño pepper, diced (optional)
3 cans (15.5 ounces each) dark red kidney beans

Method:

1. *Preheat a large stockpot over medium heat.*
2. *Use the **CRINKLE CUTTER** to chop the onion and garlic.*
3. *Use the **HERB SHEARS** to snip the green onions.*
4. *Use the **CRINKLE CUTTER** to cut the brisket into 1-inch cubes.*
5. *Use the **CRINKLE CUTTER** to dice the bacon then transfer to the stockpot.*
6. *Cook bacon until most of the fat has rendered out of it then remove the bacon and set aside.*
7. *Add 1 pound of brisket cubes to the stockpot; brown lightly on all sides then remove from stockpot.*
8. *Repeat with remaining brisket.*
9. *Place all of the brisket, bacon and remaining ingredients in the stockpot; cover, reduce heat to low and cook for 1 hour.*
10. *Taste and adjust seasoning if desired.*
11. *Garnish as desired and serve.*

SKILLET TAMALE PIE

Makes 6-8 servings

Ingredients:

1 pound ground beef or turkey
2 large yellow onions
4 garlic cloves
1-2 jalapeño peppers
1 can (7 ounces) mild green chiles
3 tablespoons chili powder
1 teaspoon ground cumin
1 can (14.5 ounces) diced tomatoes
Kosher salt and fresh pepper to taste
3 1/2 cups chicken stock
1 cup yellow cornmeal
6-ounce block Monterey Jack cheese
3 cups frozen yellow corn, thawed
Fresh cilantro

Method:

1. Preheat a large skillet over medium-high heat.
2. Add the beef to the skillet; break up the beef while browning.
3. Use the **CRINKLE CUTTER** to chop the onions, garlic and jalapeño peppers then add to the skillet.
4. Stir and cook until beef is no longer pink then add the chiles, chili powder, cumin and tomatoes; season with salt and pepper then stir.
5. In a large saucepan, bring the chicken stock to a boil over medium-high heat.
6. Add the cornmeal and whisk constantly for 2-3 minutes or until thick and bubbly; remove.
7. Use the **MEDIUM GRATER** to grate the cheese then add half to cornmeal mixture along with the corn to the saucepan; stir, season with salt and pepper then remove from heat.
8. Pour the cornmeal mixture evenly over the beef mixture then top with remaining cheese.
9. Preheat a broiler then broil for 5 minutes or until brown, bubbly and cheese has all melted.
10. Use the **HERB SHEARS** to snip cilantro for garnish before serving.

QUICK & EASY
CHICKEN DIVAN

Makes 4 servings

Ingredients:

2 tablespoons canola oil, divided
4 boneless, skinless chicken breasts
Kosher salt and fresh pepper to taste
1/2 cup all purpose flour
1 large yellow onion
1 cup strong chicken stock
3/4 cup heavy cream
3-ounce block of Parmesan cheese
2 teaspoons Worcestershire sauce
2 tablespoons brandy
1 tablespoon lemon juice
1 bag (16 ounces) frozen broccoli florets

Method:

1. *Preheat 1 tablespoon oil in a large skillet over medium heat.*
2. *Season chicken with salt and pepper then sprinkle all sides with flour.*
3. *When oil is hot, place the chicken into the skillet; cook for 5 minutes on each side or until just cooked through.*
4. *Remove chicken to a plate and set aside; add remaining oil to the skillet.*
5. *Use the **CRINKLE CUTTER** to julienne the onion.*
6. *Add the onions to the skillet and cook for 10 minutes or until browned.*
7. *Add the stock and cream to the skillet; simmer for 5 minutes.*
8. *Use the **MEDIUM GRATER** to grate the Parmesan cheese then add all but 1/3 cup of cheese to the skillet; stir.*
9. *Add the Worcestershire sauce, brandy and lemon juice; adjust seasoning if desired.*
10. *Add the broccoli to the skillet.*
11. *Return the chicken to the skillet and spoon over it some sauce and broccoli.*
12. *Top chicken with the reserved Parmesan cheese; cover and let stand for 5 minutes or until cheese is melted then garnish as desired before serving.*

BEST PAN ROASTED CHICKEN

Makes 4 servings

Ingredients:

1 whole chicken, cut into 8 pieces
1 large yellow onion
1 pound red bliss potatoes
8 fresh thyme sprigs
8 fresh sage leaves
3 tablespoons olive oil
1 tablespoon unsalted butter, melted
Kosher salt and fresh pepper to taste
1 lemon

Method:

1. *Preheat oven to 400°F.*
2. *Place the chicken pieces on a 1/2-sheet pan.*
3. *Use the **CRINKLE CUTTER** to chop the onion and cut the potatoes in half; transfer to 1/2-sheet pan.*
4. *Use the **HERB SHEARS** to snip the thyme and sage over the chicken.*
5. *Drizzle with the oil and butter then season liberally with salt and pepper.*
6. *Use the **CITRUS ZESTER** to zest the lemon over the chicken.*
7. *Use the **CRINKLE CUTTER** to cut lemon in half then squeeze over the ingredients on the 1/2-sheet pan; toss well.*
8. *Arrange all ingredients in a single layer on the 1/2-sheet pan.*
9. *Bake for 35 minutes or until food is well browned and chicken reaches 165°F on a meat thermometer.*
10. *Garnish as desired before serving.*

CHICKEN VESUVIO

Makes 4 servings

Ingredients:

1 tablespoon olive oil, divided
4 boneless, skinless chicken breasts
Kosher salt and fresh pepper to taste
4 garlic cloves
1 pound small red skinned potatoes
1 sprig fresh rosemary
2 sprigs fresh oregano
1/2 cup white wine
1 cup chicken stock
1 bag (8 ounces) frozen peas
1 lemon

Method:

1. Preheat 1/2 tablespoon oil in a large skillet over medium heat.
2. Season chicken with salt and pepper.
3. When oil is hot, add the chicken to the skillet; brown on each side for 5 minutes.
4. While chicken is browning, use the **CRINKLE CUTTER** to chop the garlic and quarter the potatoes; set aside.
5. Remove chicken to a plate then add remaining oil to the skillet.
6. Add potatoes and garlic to the skillet; season with salt and pepper and cook for 5 minutes or until golden brown.
7. Return the chicken to skillet then snip the rosemary and oregano over the chicken using the **HERB SHEARS**.
8. Add the wine and stock to the skillet; stir well then cover and cook for 10 minutes or until chicken is cooked through and potatoes are tender.
9. Add the peas to the skillet.
10. Use the **CITRUS ZESTER** to zest the lemon over the chicken.
11. Use the **CRINKLE CUTTER** to cut the lemon in half then squeeze over the chicken.
12. Stir, remove from heat and garnish as desired before serving.

ONE SKILLET CHICKEN STEW

Makes 4 servings

Ingredients:

4 boneless, skinless chicken breasts
1 large yellow onion
2 large potatoes
2 carrots
2 celery stalks

Kosher salt and fresh pepper to taste
1/2 cup all purpose flour
2 tablespoons canola oil
4 cups chicken stock
1 bay leaf

Method:

1. Use the **CRINKLE CUTTER** to cut chicken into 1-inch pieces and chop the onion.
2. Use the **Y-PEELER** to peel the potatoes and carrots.
3. Use a knife to cut the potatoes into 1/2-inch pieces, the carrots into 1/4-inch coins and the celery into 1/4-inch pieces.
4. Season chicken with salt and pepper then dredge the chicken in flour.
5. Preheat the oil in a large skillet over medium-high heat.
6. When oil is hot, add the chicken to the skillet; sear on all sides for 3-4 minutes or until browned.
7. Add the onions, potatoes, carrots, celery, stock and bay leaf; cover with lid.
8. Reduce heat to low and cook for 10-15 minutes or until chicken is tender and cooked through.
9. Garnish and adjust seasoning as desired before serving.

RECIPES

CHICKEN BOLOGNESE

Makes 6 servings

Ingredients:

1 large yellow onion
1 large carrot
1 stalk celery
1 tablespoon unsalted butter
3 tablespoons tomato paste
1/2 cup water
1 tablespoon olive oil
1 pound ground chicken thighs
Kosher salt and fresh pepper to taste
2 garlic cloves
1/4 cup dry white wine
3 cups chicken stock
1 can (28 ounces) diced tomatoes
1/2 cup whole milk
2 tablespoons heavy cream
1 pound pasta, cooked
Ricotta cheese

Method:

1. Use the **CRINKLE CUTTER** to finely chop the onion.
2. Use the **Y-PEELER** to peel the carrot.
3. Use the **CRINKLE CUTTER** to finely chop the carrot and celery.
4. Melt the butter in a large saucepot over medium heat.
5. Add the onions, carrots and celery to the saucepot then cook for about 15 minutes, stirring often, or until vegetables are brown.
6. Add the tomato paste and cook for a few additional minutes until tomato paste is browned.
7. Add the water and stir well to scrape up all the brown bits from the bottom of the pot.
8. Add the olive oil and chicken; season with salt and pepper and cook for 10 minutes.
9. Use the **CRINKLE CUTTER** to finely chop the garlic then add to the pot and stir until fragrant.
10. Add the wine, stock, tomatoes and milk; stir then adjust seasoning if desired.
11. Cover with lid then turn heat to low and simmer for 2 hours, stirring occasionally.
12. Stir in the cream and adjust seasoning if desired.
13. Serve over pasta, top with ricotta cheese and garnish as desired.

GREG'S EASY CHICKEN SOUP

Makes 2-4 servings

Ingredients:

1 tablespoon canola oil
2 carrots
1 small yellow onion
1 celery stalk
1 pound rotisserie chicken meat, cooked
1 bay leaf
1 quart chicken stock
1 cup small pasta, uncooked
Kosher salt and fresh pepper to taste

Method:

1. *Preheat the oil in a small stockpot over medium heat.*
2. *Use the **Y-PEELER** to peel the carrots.*
3. *Use the **CRINKLE CUTTER** to chop the carrots, onion, celery and chicken.*
4. *Place the carrots, onions, celery, chicken and remaining ingredients into the stockpot.*
5. *Simmer for 20-25 minutes then taste and adjust seasoning if desired.*
6. *Garnish as desired and serve.*

BBQ CHICKEN QUESADILLAS

Makes 2 servings

Ingredients:

2 flour tortillas
1/4 cup bottled BBQ sauce
1/2 cup leftover rotisserie chicken
1 small red onion
1/2 jalapeño pepper
4-ounce block Monterrey Jack cheese
2 tablespoons cilantro (optional)

Method:

1. *Preheat a large skillet over medium heat.*
2. *Place one tortilla on a cutting board and spread evenly with BBQ sauce.*
3. *Use the **CRINKLE CUTTER** to chop the chicken and thinly slice the onion and jalapeño pepper.*
4. *Use the **MEDIUM GRATER** to grate the cheese.*
5. *Top tortilla evenly with the chicken, red onions, cheese and jalapeño peppers; cover with second tortilla.*
6. *Apply nonstick spray to the skillet.*
7. *Place the quesadilla in the skillet; cook for 2 minutes on each side or until cheese is melted.*
8. *When cooking is complete, transfer the quesadilla to a cutting board then cut into wedges.*
9. *Use the **HERB SHEARS** to snip the cilantro for garnishing if desired before serving.*

CHICKEN & NOODLES

Makes 4 servings

For the Chicken:

4 boneless, skinless chicken breasts
2 large carrots
1 large yellow onion
2 celery stalks
2 tablespoons unsalted butter
4 cups good quality chicken stock
3 fresh sage leaves
2 bay leaves
Kosher salt and fresh pepper to taste
1 cup frozen peas, thawed
Mashed potatoes for serving (optional)

For the Noodles:

A handful of flat leaf parsley
1 bunch green onions
2/3 cup all purpose flour
1 large egg
1/2 teaspoon kosher salt
2 tablespoons unsalted butter, melted

Method:

1. Use the **CRINKLE CUTTER** to cut the chicken breasts into squares then transfer chicken to a large stockpot.
2. Use the **Y-PEELER** to peel the carrots then chop the carrots, onion and celery using the **CRINKLE CUTTER**; transfer to the stockpot.
3. Add the butter, stock, sage and bay leaves to the stockpot; season well with salt and pepper.
4. Set stove to medium-high heat and simmer for 20 minutes, stirring occasionally.
5. While simmering, use the **HERB SHEARS** to snip the parsley and green onions into a mixing bowl then add remaining noodle ingredients to the bowl; stir until a dough ball forms.
6. Roll out the dough on a lightly floured surface until 1/4-inch thick then use the **CRINKLE CUTTER** to cut the dough into wide noodles; transfer the noodles to the bubbling chicken mixture then cover with lid.
7. Cook noodles for 10 minutes; add the peas, stir well then adjust seasoning if desired.
8. Garnish and serve hot with mashed potatoes if desired.

EASY CHICKEN A LA KING

Makes 4 servings

Ingredients:

4 boneless, skinless chicken breasts, diced
1/2 cup heavy cream
2 1/2 teaspoons kosher salt
1 lemon
1 large yellow onion
8 ounces button mushrooms
1 garlic clove
3 tablespoons unsalted butter
3 tablespoons all purpose flour
1/3 cup Madeira wine or brandy
1 cup strong chicken stock
1 cup frozen peas, thawed
8 slices buttered toast

Method:

1. *In a bowl, combine the chicken, cream and salt.*
2. *Use the **CITRUS ZESTER** to zest the lemon over the chicken in the bowl.*
3. *Use the **CRINKLE CUTTER** to cut the lemon in half then squeeze over the chicken; stir and let marinate for 15 minutes.*
4. *Use the **CRINKLE CUTTER** to chop the onion, mushrooms and garlic.*
5. *Melt the butter in a large skillet over medium heat.*
6. *Add the onions, mushrooms and garlic; sauté for 5 minutes then add the flour; stir until smooth.*
7. *Add remaining ingredients, except toast; stir well then raise heat to medium-high.*
8. *Cook for 8-9 minutes or until chicken is just cooked through and sauce is bubbly.*
9. *Place 2 slices of toast on each serving plate, top with chicken mixture and serve.*

CHICKEN TACOS

Makes 4 servings

Ingredients:

1/4 wedge iceberg lettuce
2 Roma tomatoes
1 large red onion
1 carrot
1 jalapeño pepper
12 ounces leftover rotisserie chicken, bones removed
4-ounce block Cheddar cheese
8 taco shells
Salsa (optional)

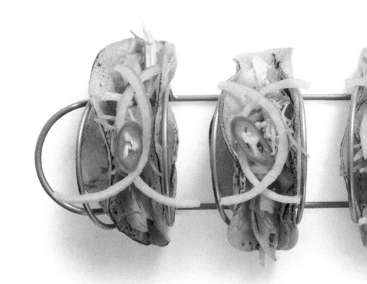

Method:

1. *Use the **CRINKLE CUTTER** to chop the lettuce and tomatoes then slice the onion.*
2. *Use the **Y-PEELER** to peel the carrot then grate it using the **MEDIUM GRATER**.*
3. *Use the **APPLE CORER** to seed the jalapeño pepper.*
4. *Use the **CRINKLE CUTTER** to slice the jalapeño pepper and chicken.*
5. *Use the **MEDIUM GRATER** to grate the cheese.*
6. *Place ingredients into the taco shells then top with cheese and salsa if desired before serving.*

CRABBY APPETIZER ROLLS

Makes 12 rolls

Ingredients:

8 ounces lump fresh crab meat (use imitation if desired)
1 bunch fresh chives
1 can (8 ounces) whole water chestnuts
1/4 red bell pepper
3 tablespoons mayonnaise
2 English cucumbers
1 teaspoon black sesame seeds

Method:

1. Place the crab meat into a bowl then remove all bits of shell.
2. Use the **HERB SHEARS** to finely snip the chives over the crab meat.
3. Use the **CRINKLE CUTTER** to chop the water chestnuts and slice the bell pepper into thin strips; add to the bowl then stir the mayonnaise into the crab mixture.
4. Use the **Y-PEELER** to peel lengthwise strips from the cucumbers.
5. Place a small spoonful of crab mixture on one end of a cucumber strip.
6. Roll it up then secure end with a small skewer; repeat to make additional rolls.
7. Sprinkle with sesame seeds before serving.

CREAM CHEESE STUFFED GRAPE APPETIZERS

Makes 6-10 servings

Ingredients:

24 large red or green grapes
1/4 cup toasted pistachio nuts, chopped
8 ounces cream cheese
2 tablespoons honey

Method:

1. Use the **CRINKLE CUTTER** to trim the bottom off each grape so they sit flat.
2. Use the **APPLE CORER** to remove the top from each grape.
3. Dip the cut side of each grape in the pistachio nuts then place the grapes on a serving tray.
4. Use the **DUAL MELON BALLER** to scoop 24 small cream cheese balls.
5. Roll each ball over a piece of cheesecloth for a decorative edge if desired.
6. Fill each grape with a cream cheese ball then drizzle with honey before serving.

SALMON & MUSHROOM
BROWN RICE

Makes 2 servings

For the Steamed Salmon:

1 green onion
2 teaspoons fresh ginger
1 garlic clove
2 salmon fillets, 4 ounces each
1 tablespoon soy sauce

For the Rice:

2/3 cup brown rice
1 1/4 cups stock or water
1 bay leaf
2 teaspoons olive oil
1/2 cup dried shiitake mushrooms (rehydrated in 1 cup hot water, squeezed to remove excess water)
2 teaspoons soy sauce
1 garlic clove, smashed
1/2 teaspoon chili flakes
Kosher salt and fresh pepper to taste
1 green onion

Method:

1. Use the **HERB SHEARS** to snip the green onion for the salmon.
2. Use the **Y-PEELER** to remove the skin from the ginger.
3. Use the **CRINKLE CUTTER** to chop the ginger and garlic.
4. Rub salmon with soy sauce.
5. Top salmon evenly with green onions, garlic and ginger; let marinate for 10 minutes.
6. Place all rice ingredients, except green onion, into a saucepan.
7. Bring to a boil over medium heat then simmer for 15 minutes before reducing heat to low.
8. Use the **HERB SHEARS** to snip the green onion for the rice.
9. Top rice with salmon and green onions; cover and cook for an additional 7 - 10 minutes or until salmon is cooked to desired doneness.
10. Garnish as desired and serve salmon over rice.

SHRIMP & GRITS

Makes 3-4 servings

For the Grits:

4 cups water
1 teaspoon kosher salt
1 cup stone ground grits
4 tablespoons butter, divided

For the Shrimp:

1 tablespoon olive oil
1 1/2 pounds large shrimp, peeled and deveined
Kosher salt and fresh pepper to taste
1 garlic clove
1 corn on the cob
1 bunch green onions for garnish
1/2 teaspoon chili flakes

Method:

1. *Pour water and salt into a stockpot; bring water to a boil over high heat.*
2. *Whisk in the grits, reduce heat to low then cover and cook for 15 minutes or until grits are tender; remove from heat, stir in 2 tablespoons butter then set aside.*
3. *Preheat the olive oil and remaining butter in a large sauté pan over medium-high heat.*
4. *Pat shrimp dry, season with salt and pepper then add to the pan; toss shrimp for 3 minutes or until heated through then remove from heat (do not overcook).*
5. *Use the **CRINKLE CUTTER** to chop the garlic and cut the corn from the cob.*
6. *Use the **HERB SHEARS** to snip the green onions.*
7. *Add the corn, garlic, chili flakes and green onions to the pan; stir and cook for 1 minute or until vegetables are soft and fragrant.*
8. *Serve grits in bowls, topped with shrimp and garlic mixture.*

SAUSAGE & SAUERKRAUT

Makes 2-4 servings

Ingredients:

1 carrot
4 small red skinned potatoes, scrubbed
1 pound kielbasa sausage
1 bag (1 pound) fresh sauerkraut, drained
1 cup beer, chicken stock or water
Fresh parsley for garnish

Method:

1. Use the **Y-PEELER** to peel the carrot.
2. Use the **CRINKLE CUTTER** to cut the carrot, potatoes and sausage into pieces.
3. Place all ingredients, except parsley, into a stockpot; cover with lid and cook over medium heat for 20 minutes or until potatoes and carrots are tender.
4. Use the **HERB SHEARS** to snip parsley for garnishing before serving.

SMOTHERED PORK CHOPS

Makes 4 servings

Ingredients:

1 bacon slice
2 large yellow onions
2 garlic cloves
4 bone-in pork chops, 6 ounces each
Kosher salt and fresh pepper to taste
1 tablespoon unsalted butter
1/4 teaspoon dried sage
4 tablespoons all purpose flour
1/3 cup whole milk
2 cups chicken stock
1 green onion
Cheesy mashed potatoes (see recipe on page 106)

Method:

1. Use the **CRINKLE CUTTER** to cut the bacon into pieces then thinly slice the onions and chop the garlic; set aside.
2. Pat pork chops thoroughly dry using paper towels then season with salt and pepper.
3. Melt the butter in a large sauté pan over medium-high heat.
4. When butter sizzles, add the pork chops, bacon, onions and garlic to the pan.
5. Sear pork on both sides until brown then add remaining ingredients, except green onion and mashed potatoes; cover and reduce heat to low then simmer for 1 hour or until pork chops are tender.
6. Adjust seasoning if desired then use the **HERB SHEARS** to snip green onion for garnish.
7. Serve hot over mashed potatoes.

PORK STEW

Makes 4-6 servings

Ingredients:

2 whole carrots
2 small sweet potatoes
1 large yellow onion
1 celery stalk
4 garlic cloves
1 tablespoon canola oil
4 pounds pork shoulder, cubed
Kosher salt and fresh pepper to taste
4 cups good quality chicken stock
2 teaspoons minute tapioca
1 bay leaf
2 tablespoons ketchup
12 ounces beer or chicken stock
Parsley for garnish

Method:

1. Use the **Y-PEELER** to peel the carrots and potatoes then chop the carrots, potatoes, onion, celery and garlic using the **CRINKLE CUTTER**.
2. Preheat the oil in a Dutch oven over medium-high heat.
3. When oil is hot, add the pork and sear on all sides until browned; season with salt and pepper.
4. Add remaining ingredients, except parsley, to the Dutch oven; stir well then turn heat to low.
5. Simmer for 2 hours or until pork is tender.
6. Adjust seasoning if desired then snip parsley over the stew using the **HERB SHEARS** before serving.

WOLF'S REISFLEISCH

Makes 6 servings

Ingredients:

1 large carrot
1 large yellow onion
1 garlic clove
1 celery stalk
1 bell pepper, any color
1 pound smoked sausage
4 tablespoons unsalted butter

2 cups uncooked long grain rice
4 cups chicken stock
2 teaspoons fresh lemon juice
1 tablespoon paprika
Kosher salt and fresh pepper to taste
Chili flakes to taste
Fresh parsley

Method:

1. Use the **Y-PEELER** to peel the carrot then chop the carrot, onion, garlic, celery, bell pepper and sausage; set aside.
2. Melt the butter in a large stockpot over medium heat.
3. When butter is melted, add the rice and stir to coat for 3 minutes.
4. Add remaining ingredients, except parsley; stir well, reduce heat to low and cover with lid.
5. Cook for 20-25 minutes or until rice is done.
6. Remove from heat then use the **HERB SHEARS** to snip the parsley for garnish.
7. Fluff rice and serve hot.

SAUSAGE & CHEESE CASSEROLE

Makes 4-6 servings

Ingredients:

1 pound breakfast sausage
1 small yellow onion
1/2 loaf Italian bread
2 Russet potatoes
4 sprigs fresh parsley
1 green bell pepper
1 tablespoon unsalted butter, softened
6 large eggs, beaten
Kosher salt and fresh pepper to taste
3 cups half & half
1 teaspoon apple cider vinegar
4 ounce block sharp Cheddar cheese
1 ounce block Parmesan cheese

Method:

1. Use the **CRINKLE CUTTER** to slice the sausage.
2. Preheat a large skillet over medium heat; add the sausage to brown.
3. Use the **CRINKLE CUTTER** to chop the onion then add to the skillet.
4. Use the **CRINKLE CUTTER** to cube the bread then add to the skillet.
5. Use the **CRINKLE CUTTER** to cube the potatoes then add to the skillet.
6. Use the **HERB SHEARS** to snip the parsley over the skillet (reserve some parsley for garnish).
7. Use the **CRINKLE CUTTER** to chop the bell pepper then add to the skillet.
8. Add the butter, eggs, salt, pepper, half & half and vinegar; stir gently, pushing the eggs from the edge to the center, allowing the liquid part of the egg to flow under the cooked part.
9. Reduce heat to low and continue to cook until mixture is mostly set; remove from heat.
10. Use the **MEDIUM GRATER** to grate both cheeses.
11. Add cheeses to the skillet, cover and cook for 5 minutes or until melted.
12. Garnish with additional parsley before serving.

SWEET & SOUR PORK

Makes 4-6 servings

Ingredients:

2 carrots
1 medium yellow onion
3 garlic cloves
2 tablespoons fresh ginger
6 tablespoons rice wine vinegar
4 tablespoons ketchup
6 tablespoons sugar
6 tablespoons soy sauce
1 tablespoon cornstarch
1 can (15.25 ounces) tropical mixed fruit (pineapple, papaya, peaches), juice reserved
2 tablespoons canola oil
1 pound pork loin chop
Cooked rice for serving (optional)

Method:

1. Use the **Y-PEELER** to peel the carrots.
2. Use the **CRINKLE CUTTER** to chop the carrots, onion, garlic and ginger.
3. In a bowl, whisk together the vinegar, ketchup, sugar, soy sauce, cornstarch and 1/3 cup of juice from the tropical mixed fruit can; set aside.
4. Preheat the oil in a large sauté pan over high heat.
5. Pat the pork dry using paper towels then cut into 1/4-inch strips using the **CRINKLE CUTTER**.
6. When oil is hot, place half of the pork into the pan and cook for 1-2 minutes on each side or until well browned; transfer to a bowl then repeat with remaining pork.
7. Add the onions, carrots, garlic and ginger to the pan; cook for 4 minutes.
8. Add the fruit juice mixture, tropical mixed fruit and pork to the pan; stir to combine then cook for 2-3 minutes or until thickened.
9. When cooking is complete, remove from pan and serve over rice if desired.

SKINNY CHIPS & SALSA

Makes 6 servings

Ingredients:

6 large ripe tomatoes
1 garlic clove
1 large white onion
1-2 serrano chili peppers
A handful of fresh cilantro
2 limes
1 jicama bulb
2 English cucumbers

Method:

1. Use the **CRINKLE CUTTER** to chop the tomatoes, garlic, onion and chili peppers; transfer to a bowl.
2. Use the **HERB SHEARS** to snip the cilantro over the tomato mixture.
3. Use the **CITRUS ZESTER** to zest the limes into the bowl then cut limes in half and squeeze juice into the bowl.
4. Use the **Y-PEELER** to peel the jicama then cut the jicama and cucumber into "chips" using the **CRINKLE CUTTER**.
5. Serve salsa with cucumber and jicama chips.

ZUCCHINI LATKES

Makes 4 servings

Ingredients:

2 cups zucchini, raw
1/2 cup yellow onion
1/4 cup celery leaves
3 green onions
3 large eggs
1/3 cup all purpose flour
Kosher salt and fresh pepper to taste
3 tablespoons canola oil
Sour cream for serving

Method:

1. Use the **MEDIUM GRATER** to grate the zucchini and onion then pat dry thoroughly using paper towels.
2. Use the **HERB SHEARS** to snip the celery leaves and green onions.
3. Preheat a large skillet over medium heat.
4. In a bowl, stir together the zucchini, onions, celery, green onions, eggs, flour, salt and pepper.
5. Brush skillet with some of the oil then drop mounds of zucchini mixture into the skillet.
6. Cook for 2-3 minutes on each side or until well browned.
7. Remove and repeat with any remaining mixture then serve hot with sour cream.

BUTTERNUT SQUASH SOUP

Makes 6 servings

Ingredients:

1 large yellow onion
2 tablespoons unsalted butter
1 tablespoon olive oil
2 pounds butternut squash, cubed
3 cups chicken stock
2 teaspoons apple cider vinegar
2 teaspoons kosher salt
1/2 teaspoon fresh pepper
1/2 teaspoon ground cinnamon
1 cup half & half or milk
Chives for garnish
1 tablespoon honey

Method:

1. *Use the **CRINKLE CUTTER** to chop the onion.*
2. *In an 8 quart stockpot over medium heat, melt the butter and heat the oil.*
3. *Add the onions and cook for 5 minutes or until translucent.*
4. *Add the butternut squash, chicken stock, vinegar, salt, pepper and cinnamon; cover with lid.*
5. *Reduce heat to medium-low and let simmer for 30 minutes or until butternut squash is fork tender.*
6. *Transfer 1/3 of the squash mixture to a blender; cover with lid.*
7. *Puree on low speed to avoid splashing then increase speed to high and puree until smooth.*
8. *Pour into a serving tureen and repeat with remaining squash mixture.*
9. *Add the half & half or milk; stir until combined.*
10. *Ladle into bowls.*
11. *Use the **HERB SHEARS** to snip the chives for garnish.*
12. *Drizzle soup with honey before serving.*

QUINOA PILAF

Makes 6 servings

For the Quinoa:

1 small yellow onion
1/2 cup dried apricots
2 cups quinoa
1 3/4 cups water
1 tablespoon chicken bouillon powder
1 tablespoon soy sauce
2 tablespoons olive oil
1/2 teaspoon dried thyme
1 cup sliced almonds, toasted
1 cup raisins
1/2 teaspoon chili flakes or to taste

For Serving:

1 bunch green onions
2 tablespoons parsley
1 lemon
1 cup red grapes
Kosher salt and fresh pepper to taste

Method:

1. Use the **CRINKLE CUTTER** to chop the onion and apricots.
2. Preheat a stockpot over medium-high heat.
3. Using a fine strainer, rinse the quinoa for 1 minute to remove the bitter natural coating.
4. Place all quinoa ingredients into the stockpot; cover with lid and cook for 15 minutes.
5. While quinoa is cooking, use the **HERB SHEARS** to snip the green onions and parsley.
6. Use the **CITRUS ZESTER** to zest the lemon then cut lemon in half and squeeze the juice into a small bowl.
7. Use the **CRINKLE CUTTER** to cut the grapes in half.
8. When cooking is complete, add all ingredients for serving to the stockpot; stir.
9. Taste and adjust seasoning if desired.
10. Serve hot or cold.

MAC & CHEESE

Makes 6 servings

Ingredients:

5-ounce block mozzarella cheese
6-ounce block extra sharp Cheddar cheese
2-ounce block Monterey Jack cheese
2-ounce wedge of Parmesan cheese
1 cup Cheddar cheese for topping
7 cups elbow or other small pasta, cooked
1/2 cup chicken stock
1/2 cup half & half
1 tablespoon unsalted butter
1 teaspoon dry mustard
Pinch of cayenne pepper
1 teaspoon kosher salt or to taste
1 tablespoon ketchup
Chives for garnish

Method:

1. *Use the **MEDIUM GRATER** to grate all the cheeses; set aside 1 cup Cheddar cheese for topping.*
2. *Preheat oven to 350°F.*
3. *In a bowl, combine all ingredients, except chives and reserved Cheddar cheese; gently stir to combine.*
4. *Divide the mixture between small casserole dishes or cocottes then top with reserved cheese.*
5. *Bake for 30-40 minutes or until bubbly and top is golden brown.*
6. *Use the **HERB SHEARS** to snip chives for garnishing before serving.*

VEGETARIAN OMELET POCKETS

Makes 2 servings

Ingredients:

2-ounce block Parmesan cheese
1 small yellow onion
2 tablespoons mushrooms
1/2 red bell pepper
8 spinach leaves
4 large eggs
Kosher salt and fresh pepper to taste

Method:

1. *Use the **MEDIUM GRATER** to grate the Parmesan cheese.*
2. *Use the **CRINKLE CUTTER** to slice the onion, mushrooms and bell pepper.*
3. *Use the **HERB SHEARS** to julienne the spinach.*
4. *Preheat an omelet pan over medium heat.*
5. *In a bowl, whisk the eggs then season with salt and pepper.*
6. *Apply nonstick spray to the pan then add the eggs.*
7. *Use a spatula to lift the edges as it cooks while moving the pan back and forth.*
8. *Top omelet with vegetables and cheese then fold in half and serve.*

VEGGIE & PASTA SALAD

Makes 4 servings

Ingredients:

1/2 cup fresh spinach
1/4 cup green onions
1 small yellow onion
1 cup cherry tomatoes
4 cups shell or other pasta, cooked
2 tablespoons olive oil
2 tablespoons balsamic vinegar
Kosher salt and fresh pepper to taste

Method:

1. *Use the **HERB SHEARS** to julienne the spinach and snip the green onions.*
2. *Use the **CRINKLE CUTTER** to chop the yellow onion and slice the tomatoes in half.*
3. *Place all ingredients into a large bowl; toss gently to combine.*
4. *Adjust seasoning if desired and serve.*

HOT CHILI PEPPER FLOWERS

For Garnishing

Ingredients:

Assorted long, thin chili peppers in various colors

Method:

1. *Wash the peppers wearing kitchen gloves if you are sensitive to chili heat.*
2. *Use the **CRINKLE CUTTER** to make thin cuts from the chili stem to the tip.*
3. *Place the peppers in ice water for 4 hours or until peppers open up.*
4. *Use the chili pepper flowers to decorate desired foods.*

SCALLOPED CORN

Makes 8 servings

Ingredients:

3 corn on the cob
3 green onions
2-ounce block Parmesan cheese
3 large eggs, beaten
20 saltine crackers, crushed
1 cup half & half
2 teaspoons sugar
2 teaspoons kosher salt
Pepper to taste

Method:

1. *Preheat oven to 350°F.*
2. *Use the **CRINKLE CUTTER** to remove the corn kernels from the cobs.*
3. *Use the **HERB SHEARS** to snip the green onions.*
4. *Use the **MEDIUM GRATER** to grate the Parmesan cheese.*
5. *Combine all ingredients in a large bowl; mix well then pour into a greased casserole dish.*
6. *Bake for 45 minutes or until well browned; garnish as desired and serve.*

SEVEN LAYER SALAD

Makes 6 servings

Ingredients:

1 head iceberg lettuce
1/2 red onion
1 small cucumber
2 cups frozen peas, thawed
1 cup mayonnaise
1 tablespoon sugar
1 tablespoon yellow mustard
4-ounce block of Cheddar cheese
8 bacon slices, cooked and crumbled

Method:

1. *Use the **CRINKLE CUTTER** to chop the lettuce then transfer to an 8 x 8-inch glass dish; firmly press the lettuce to the bottom of the glass dish.*
2. *Use the **CRINKLE CUTTER** to dice the onion and cucumber then press into the glass dish and top with peas.*
3. *In a bowl, whisk together the mayonnaise, sugar and mustard; spoon mixture into the glass dish then use the **MEDIUM GRATER** to grate the Cheddar cheese over the mayonnaise mixture.*
4. *Top with bacon then chill before serving.*

SOUTHERN POTATO SALAD

Makes 4 servings

Ingredients:

2 pounds red skinned potatoes
1/2 small yellow onion
1 celery stalk
1 tablespoon apple cider vinegar
2 tablespoons sweet pickle relish
1/2 cup mayonnaise
2 tablespoons yellow mustard
Kosher salt and fresh pepper to taste

Method:

1. *Fill a stockpot with enough water to cover the potatoes; bring to a boil.*
2. *Use the **CRINKLE CUTTER** to cut the potatoes into 1/2-inch cubes.*
3. *Place potatoes in the stockpot and cook for 20 minutes or until potatoes are tender; drain.*
4. *While potatoes are cooking, use the **CRINKLE CUTTER** to dice the onion and celery.*
5. *In a large bowl, combine potatoes and remaining ingredients; toss well.*
6. *Serve immediately or chill until serving time.*

CHEESY MASHED POTATOES

Makes 4 servings

Ingredients:

6 large Russet potatoes
5 quarts water
Kosher salt to taste
4 tablespoons unsalted butter, melted and hot
1 cup whole milk or half & half, hot
Cheddar cheese
Chives

Method:

1. *Use the **Y-PEELER** to peel the potatoes then cut into cubes using the **CRINKLE CUTTER**.*
2. *Place the potatoes and water into a large stockpot over medium-high heat; season with salt.*
3. *Cook for 20 minutes or until potatoes are fork tender; drain.*
4. *Mash potatoes with butter and salt to taste then stir in enough hot milk until soft and creamy or until desired consistency; taste and adjust seasoning if desired.*
5. *Use the **MEDIUM GRATER** to grate the Cheddar cheese over the potatoes then use the **HERB SHEARS** to snip the chives for garnish before serving.*

GRANDMA'S LEMON BARS

Makes 12-18 bars

For the Crust:

1 1/2 cups all purpose flour
1/4 cup powdered sugar
1/2 cup unsalted butter, melted

For the Lemon Filling:

6 lemons
4 eggs
1 1/4 cups sugar
2 tablespoons all purpose flour
1/2 teaspoon kosher salt
1/2 teaspoon vanilla extract

Method:

1. *Preheat oven to 350°F.*
2. *Stir all crust ingredients together in a 9 x 9-inch pan; press the dough into the bottom.*
3. *Bake for 15-20 minutes or until light golden brown; remove and set aside.*
4. *Use the **CITRUS ZESTER** to zest 1 lemon into a bowl.*
5. *Use the **CRINKLE CUTTER** to cut lemons in half then squeeze 1/2 cup of juice into the bowl.*
6. *Add remaining filling ingredients to the bowl; whisk then pour over the hot crust.*
7. *Return to the oven and bake for 20-25 minutes or until filling is set (do not over bake); serve.*

FRESH MANGO SORBET

Makes about 1 quart

Ingredients:

4 large, very ripe mangoes
1 lime
1/2 - 2/3 cup granulated sugar (more or less depending on sweetness of mangoes)
Tiny pinch of kosher salt
Honeydew melon

Method:

1. *Use the **Y-PEELER** to peel the mangoes then cube them using the **CRINKLE CUTTER**.*
2. *Use the **CITRUS ZESTER** to zest the lime then use the **CRINKLE CUTTER** to cut lime in half and squeeze the juice into a bowl.*
3. *Use an blender to puree all ingredients, except melon; strain if desired.*
4. *Chill until very cold then spin in an ice cream maker following manufacturer's instructions.*
5. *Use the **DUAL MELON BALLER** to scoop balls from the honeydew melon for garnish.*

BROWN SUGAR BAKED APPLES

Makes 4 servings

Ingredients:
4 Pink Lady apples
4 tablespoons unsalted butter, divided
4 tablespoons dark brown sugar, packed
1/2 cup coconut flakes, toasted
1/2 cup cream of coconut
1 1/4 cups apple cider

Method:
1. Preheat oven to 350°F.
2. If apples do not stand up straight, trim off the bottoms using the **CRINKLE CUTTER**.
3. Use the **DUAL MELON BALLER** to remove the core and create a pocket (do not scoop all the way to the bottom of the apples) then place the apples in a baking dish.
4. Divide the butter, brown sugar, coconut flakes and cream of coconut between the apples.
5. Pour apple cider down the side of the baking dish; cover baking dish with aluminum foil.
6. Bake for 1 hour or until apples are tender then remove and serve warm.

LEMON TART WITH MANGO RIBBONS

Makes 6 servings

Ingredients:
1 package refrigerated pie crust
1 jar store-bought lemon curd
1 lime
2 firm mangoes, unpeeled

Method:
1. Preheat oven to 350°F and grease a fluted tart pan.
2. Unroll the pie crust dough then ease onto the tart pan without stretching.
3. Press the dough evenly up the sides of the pan.
4. Bake for 25-30 minutes or until brown around the edges; remove and let cool.
5. Fill cooled tart with lemon curd then use the **CITRUS ZESTER** to zest the lime over the top.
6. Use the **CRINKLE CUTTER** to cut 4 even wedges from each of the mangoes.
7. Use the **Y-PEELER** to slice long, thin, even "ribbons" from the mango wedges.
8. Roll up each "ribbon" into a coil then arrange decoratively on top of the lemon curd before serving.

SOURCE PAGE

Here are some of my favorite places to find ingredients that are not readily available at grocery stores as well as kitchen tools and supplies that help you become a better cook.

The Bakers Catalogue at King Arthur Flour

135 Route 5 South
P.O. Box 1010
Norwich, VT 05055

Pure fruit oils, citric acid, silicone spatulas, digital timers, oven thermometers, real truffle oil, off-set spatulas, measuring cups and spoons, knives, ice cream scoops, cheesecloth, cookie sheets, baking pans
www.kingarthurflour.com

D & G Occasions

625 Herndon Ave.
Orlando, FL 32803
407-894-4458

My favorite butter vanilla extract by Magic Line, cake and candy making supplies, citric acid, pure fruit oils, professional food colorings, ultra thin flexible spatulas, large selection of sprinkles and jimmies, unusual birthday candles, pure vanilla extract, pastry bags and tips, parchment, off-set spatulas, oven and candy thermometers, kitchen timers, meat mallets, large selection of cookie cutters, googly eyes
www.dandgoccasions.com

Chocosphere

P.O. Box 2237
Tualatin, OR 97062
877-992-4623

Excellent quality cocoa (Callebaut)
All Chocolates
Jimmies and sprinkles
www.chocosphere.com

Gluten Free Mall

4927 Sonoma HWY Suite C1
Santa Rosa, CA 95409
707-509-4528

All ingredients needed for gluten-free baking
www.glutenfreemall.com

Penzeys Spices

P.O. Box 924
Brookfield, WI 53045
800-741-7787

Spices, extracts, seasonings, seasonal cookie cutters, mallets and more
www.penzeys.com

INDEX